36 Texas Instruments TI-99/4A Programs for Home, School & Office

36 Texas Instruments TI-99/4A Programs for Home, School & Office

by Len Turner

ARCsoft Publishers
WOODSBORO, MARYLAND

FIRST EDITION
THIRD PRINTING

© 1983 by ARCsoft Publishers, P.O. Box 132, Woodsboro, MD 21798 USA

Library of Congress (LC) number: 83-5989

ISBN 0-86668-024-1

Preface

The Texas Instruments microcomputers are among the world's most popular systems for use in the home, classroom and small-business office. In fact, the TI-99/4A probably is the all-time best-selling home computer to date.

The lightweight desktop design of the TI-99/4A, the convenient portability of the Compact 40, the powerful BASIC language capability of all the TI microcomputers place them in the forefront of the new wave of personal computers for hobbyists, students, teachers, professionals, business persons and all who want to learn the new technology.

These are not toys! Their hardware and software combinations make them highly useful tools in the business environment and the classroom as well as for practical jobs around the home.

The total number of applications to which the Texas Instruments home, personal and business microcomputers can be put is limited only by the scope of the imagination. In this book, we have attempted to create and share three dozen new specific practical sets of applications programs for your use.

This book, as well as all published by *ARCsoft Publishers*, is written for newcomers, novices and first-timers, as well as for advanced users of microcomputers. Our intention has been to provide easy-to-type-in-and-run programs for the Texas Instruments TI-99/4A, TI-99/2, Compact 40, and other TI personal, home and business microcomputers. You type these programs into your computer and it does the rest. You do not have to be a program writer to use this book!

This volume is a companion book to *101 Programming Tips & Tricks for the Texas Instruments TI-99/4A Home Computer* and the *Texas Instruments Computer Program Writing Workbook*.

—Len Turner

Table of Contents

Programs for the business person

Introduction

There is a great need for practical, useful software for the new generation of popular personal computers. The Texas Instruments models TI-99/4A Home Computer, TI-99/2 computer, Compact 40 portable computer, and other TI personal/home/business microcomputers, for instance, are among the world's most popular gear. The TI computers are powerful and versatile and flexible—but what can they do? Once you've purchased the hardware, you need down-to-earth workable programs to run the computer.

The aim of this book is to provide three dozen complete easy-to-type-in ready-to-run new and different sets of program listings for you to use in your own TI, to make your computer work for you.

These programs are very useful in themselves. They also make good starting points for further development as you learn more and more about how to program your own computer. You can learn a great deal about how BASIC programs are organized and how they work simply by typing in these programs. Use these fun and practical programs and, then, modify them and expand them to suit your needs as your interests grow.

These programs are designed to be typed into your computer, via its keyboard console, just as you find the programs printed here in this book. No other programming is needed. We assume you have read the owner's manuals and instructional pamphlets which came with your computer and accessories. You know how to hook up the console to the TV modulator/connector and to any other accessories you may have purchased. You know how to type the programs into your TI computer. You *do not have to be a programmer* to use these pieces of software. Just type them in, as you find them here, and run them. They will work!

These programs do not require tape or disk, unless you choose to save them on those media. These programs are so easy to type in you can save this book and retype them whenever you wish to rerun a program.

Computer printouts

To make sure there are no errors in these programs, we have written and tested each and every program on our own TI-99/4A *and* printed every one on a TI-99 line printer. The hardcopy printout from that line printer is reproduced directly in this book!

The TI computer operated the printer and listed these programs. No human hands came between the computer and these listings so no re-typing or proofreading errors have been introduced. You should find these programs run exactly as reproduced here.

If, after typing in a program from this book, you get an error message from your TI computer, compare your typed program lines with the program lines reproduced in this book.

Undoubtedly, you will find you have made a typing error in entering the program lines into your TI. However, should you find an error in a program in this book, please call it to the attention of the author by sending a postcard or letter to him in care of *ARCsoft Publishers*, P.O. Box 132, Woodsboro, MD 21798 USA. The author will appreciate being able to make any necessary corrections to future editions of this book.

Home, school and office

This book has been organized into three sections.

The first section includes programs which might be useful in the home and wherever hobbyists use a computer. The second section includes programs for use in a learning environment, by students, teachers and parents. This might be a classroom or it might be in your home. The third section holds programs of interest to business persons and professionals.

Naturally, these sections, as divided up in the book, are not rigid and exclusive. You probably will find something in the business or classroom section of the book applicable to your home use. And you probably will take several of the home programs to your office or classroom.

Try them all. They're great fun to run. And they are especially designed to be short so you won't have to spend hours typing in one program.

Endless running

Many of the programs in this book will continue to run until you command them off manually via the CLEAR function. You may stop any run, at any time, by use of the CLEAR function. For example, *Poetrywriter* will continue to generate new and different verses until you use the CLEAR function.

The function key is in the lower right corner of the console keyboard and is labeled FCTN. Press and hold FCTN and press the number 4 key in the upper row of keys. The combination of FCTN and 4 creates the CLEAR instruction to the computer.

This CLEAR function is the same as what is called BREAK in other microcomputers.

Here is an example of how the CLEAR function works in the TI computer. Type in this brief two-line program. Type in line 10 and press ENTER. Then type in line 20 and press ENTER. This will lodge the complete program in program memory. Here is the program:

```
10 PRINT "XYZ"
20 GOTO 10
```

After you have the program stored in program memory, type in RUN and press ENTER to start the operation. The computer will do as instructed. It will print the letters XYZ repeatedly. In fact, it will go on forever until you stop the action.

To stop the run, press and hold the FCTN key. While holding FCTN down, press the number 4 key. This is the CLEAR function. It will stop the computer run. Try it.

REMarks

As you read through all of the programs in this book, you will notice few REM, or remarks, statements. The author's training in writing BASIC-language computer programs included an emphasis on brevity and saving of memory space. A sharp editing pencil was in order—and still is!

REMarks and explanations in software are out. Honing, fine tuning, and waste trimming are in. Use of coding-form program-writing worksheets is encouraged. Such worksheets can be found in the *Texas Instrument Program Writing Workbook* published by *ARCsoft Publishers*. Your objective always should be to make the most efficient use of available memory.

Always remember: even though they may be headed toward the same goal, no two programmers will write the exact same list of BASIC instructions, or program lines, from scratch. As you load these various programs into your TI computer, one at a time, you'll make modifications to suit your personal needs and interests. For instance, exact wording of PRINT statements can be changed. Or two or more programs can be combined into one grand scheme. Your applications may vary.

If you want to load more than one of these programs into your TI computer at the same time, be sure to use different sets of line numbers for different programs.

Computer programmers today generally mix the use of the two words, ENTER and RETURN. They are used to mean the same thing. In this case, we mean the ENTER key on the right side of the console keyboard.

Other computers

These programs will run on any computer which is set up to be programmed in BASIC. However, to run these on machines other than ones using TI BASIC as found in the TI-99/4A, you may have to make slight modifications to program lines. Graphic commands, especially, will differ elsewhere. Also use of multiple-statement lines, using the colon (:), is quite different in most other forms of BASIC.

Refer to the owner's manual which came with your non-TI personal computer. Compare its version of BASIC with TI BASIC.

Also, if you use a non-TI microcomputer, such things as line numbering, spacing, logical tests, multiplication symbols, print statements and other instructions may differ.

The author would like to have your suggestions for changes in future editions of this work, or for other titles in this series for the TI computers. The author may be addressed in care of *ARCsoft Publishers*.

Standalone vs. subroutine

All of the programs in this book can be used as portions of larger lists of instructions to your computer. That is, they can be written in as GOTO or GOSUB objects. To do so, make appropriate changes to the first line (usually numbered 10 in this book) and the last line of each program.

If you create a subroutine, remember that every GOSUB must have a RETURN. RETURN must be the last line of each subroutine.

If you work one of these programs into a larger set of instructions, be especially careful of your memory (variable) names or labels. They must agree with, and fit into, those you are using in the main program. Also, be careful of line numbers. No two programs can occupy the exact same set of line numbers.

If you want to load more than one of these programs into your TI computer at the same time, be sure to use different sets of line numbers.

Learning programming

These programs are written to be typed into your TI computer just as you find them here with no programming needed. We assume you know how to turn on your computer and how to go about typing in a program. Many of the programs and much of the programming advice in this book will, in fact, also be of interest to old-timers in the program-writing game since we have presented many powerful new twists aimed at making your computer do more work more quickly.

Amidst the three dozen programs in this book, you will find countless ideas for using your computer. Each program is intended to make you a more-versatile programmer and make your programming chores lighter.

Use this book to stimulate your thinking about how to approach various software problems and projects. Use it to get good ideas for new and different approaches to all of your programming goals. As you grow and develop as a program writer, modify these programs and make your computer do even more.

Happy programming!

```
 ! "#$%&'()*+,-./0123456789:;<=>?@ABCDEF
! "#$%&'()*+,-./0123456789:;<=>?@ABCDEF(
"#$%&'()*+,-./0123456789:;<=>?@ABCDEFG
#$%&'()*+,-./0123456789:;<=>?@ABCDEFGH
$%&'()*+,-./0123456789:;<=>?@ABCDEFGHI
%&'()*+,-./0123456789:;<=>?@ABCDEFGHIJ
&'()*+,-./0123456789:;<=>?@ABCDEFGHIJK
'()*+,-./0123456789:;<=>?@ABCDEFGHIJKL
()*+,-./0123456789:;<=>?@ABCDEFGHIJKLM
)*+,-./0123456789:;<=>?@ABCDEFGHIJKLMN
*+,-./0123456789:;<=>?@ABCDEFGHIJKLMNO
+,-./0123456789:;<=>?@ABCDEFGHIJKLMNOP
,-./0123456789:;<=>?@ABCDEFGHIJKLMNOPQ
-./0123456789:;<=>?@ABCDEFGHIJKLMNOPQRS
./0123456789:;<=>?@ABCDEFGHIJKLMNOPQRST
/0123456789:;<=>?@ABCDEFGHIJKLMNOPQRSTU
0123456789:;<=>?@ABCDEFGHIJKLMNOPQRSTU
123456789:;<=>?@ABCDEFGHIJKLMNOPQRSTUV
23456789:;<=>?@ABCDEFGHIJKLMNOPQRSTUVW
3456789:;<=>?@ABCDEFGHIJKLMNOPQRSTUVWX
456789:;<=>?@ABCDEFGHIJKLMNOPQRSTUVWXY
56789:;<=>?@ABCDEFGHIJKLMNOPQRSTUVWXYZ
6789:;<=>?@ABCDEFGHIJKLMNOPQRSTUVWXYZ[
789:;<=>?@ABCDEFGHIJKLMNOPQRSTUVWXYZ[\
89:;<=>?@ABCDEFGHIJKLMNOPQRSTUVWXYZ[\]
9:;<=>?@ABCDEFGHIJKLMNOPQRSTUVWXYZ[\]^
:;<=>?@ABCDEFGHIJKLMNOPQRSTUVWXYZ[\]^_
;<=>?@ABCDEFGHIJKLMNOPQRSTUVWXYZ[\]^_`
<=>?@ABCDEFGHIJKLMNOPQRSTUVWXYZ[\]^_`a
=>?@ABCDEFGHIJKLMNOPQRSTUVWXYZ[\]^_`ab
>?@ABCDEFGHIJKLMNOPQRSTUVWXYZ[\]^_`abc
?@ABCDEFGHIJKLMNOPQRSTUVWXYZ[\]^_`abcd
@ABCDEFGHIJKLMNOPQRSTUVWXYZ[\]^_`abcde
ABCDEFGHIJKLMNOPQRSTUVWXYZ[\]^_`abcdef
BCDEFGHIJKLMNOPQRSTUVWXYZ[\]^_`abcdefg
CDEFGHIJKLMNOPQRSTUVWXYZ[\]^_`abcdefgh
DEFGHIJKLMNOPQRSTUVWXYZ[\]^_`abcdefghi
EFGHIJKLMNOPQRSTUVWXYZ[\]^_`abcdefghij
FGHIJKLMNOPQRSTUVWXYZ[\]^_`abcdefghijk
GHIJKLMNOPQRSTUVWXYZ[\]^_`abcdefghijkl
HIJKLMNOPQRSTUVWXYZ[\]^_`abcdefghijklm
IJKLMNOPQRSTUVWXYZ[\]^_`abcdefghijklmn
```

Programs for the home

Horoscope

This fun program will entertain your family and friends for hours. It makes a great party game, too.

The player, or user, talks with the computer, giving his name, month of birth and date of birth. The computer then tells the player his sign of the zodiac and what it means. The computer describes the player's personality and predicts the player's future.

If you find the program a bit long to type in, shorten it by using the sign-of-the-zodiac response only. For instance, between lines 700 and 790 you could delete 710 and 750 or 720 to 750. That would make the program shorter and easier to type in, but without most of the exciting description.

Try it. You'll like it!

Program Listing

```
10 CALL CLEAR
20 INPUT "WHAT'S YOUR NAME?":N$
30 CALL CLEAR
40 PRINT "HI, ";N$;", NICE TO MEET YOU"
50 PRINT
60 INPUT "IN WHAT MONTH WERE YOU BORN?":M$
70 PRINT M$;" IS A NICE MONTH"
80 PRINT "WHAT DATE IN ";M$
90 INPUT D
100 CALL CLEAR
200 IF M$="DECEMBER" THEN 700
210 IF M$="JANUARY" THEN 800
220 IF M$="FEBRUARY" THEN 900
230 IF M$="MARCH" THEN 1000
240 IF M$="APRIL" THEN 1100
250 IF M$="MAY" THEN 1200
260 IF M$="JUNE" THEN 1300
270 IF M$="JULY" THEN 1400
280 IF M$="AUGUST" THEN 1500
290 IF M$="SEPTEMBER" THEN 1600
300 IF M$="OCTOBER" THEN 1700
310 IF M$="NOVEMBER" THEN 1800
```

```
320 GOTO 60
500 PRINT
510 PRINT
520 INPUT "TO DO ANOTHER, PRESS ENTER":KY$
530 GOTO 10
700 IF D<22 THEN 1810
710 PRINT "SO, ";N$;" YOU'RE A CAPRICORN"
720 PRINT "CAPRICORN IS THE GOAT"
730 PRINT
740 PRINT "YOU ARE TOUGH HEAD-TO-HEAD."
750 PRINT "YOU MISTRUST PEOPLE BUT"
760 PRINT "YOU LIKE SMALL CHILDREN."
770 PRINT
780 PRINT "YOU WILL TAKE A TRIP!"
790 GOTO 500
800 IF D<20 THEN 710
810 PRINT "SO, ";N$;" YOU ARE AN AQUARIUS"
820 PRINT "AQUARIUS IS THE WATER BEARER"
830 PRINT "YOU ARE A LIQUID PERSON,"
840 PRINT "YOU DO SNEAKY THINGS BUT"
850 PRINT "PEOPLE SECRETLY ADMIRE YOU."
860 PRINT "YOU SOON WILL FIND A REWARD!"
870 GOTO 500
900 IF D<19 THEN 810
910 PRINT "SO, ";N$;", YOU ARE A PISCES"
920 PRINT "PISCES IS THE FISH"
930 PRINT "YOU OFTEN FEEL WEAK BUT"
940 PRINT "PEOPLE THINK YOU OTHERWISE."
950 PRINT
960 PRINT "A STRANGER SOON"
970 PRINT "WILL AFFECT YOUR LIFE!"
980 GOTO 500
1000 IF D<21 THEN 910
1010 PRINT "SO, ";N$;", YOU ARE AN ARIES"
1020 PRINT "(NOT THE CAR, STUPID!)"
1030 PRINT "ARIES IS THE RAM"
1040 PRINT
1050 PRINT "YOU SOMETIMES FEEL DEVILISH"
1060 PRINT "BUT OTHERS THINK OF YOU"
1070 PRINT "AS A SAINT."
1080 PRINT "AVOID MOUNTAINS AND CAVES!"
1090 GOTO 500
```

```
1100 IF D<20 THEN 1010
1110 PRINT "SO, ";N$;", YOU ARE TAURUS"
1120 PRINT "TAURUS IS THE BULL."
1130 PRINT
1140 PRINT "MOST OF THE TIME"
1150 PRINT "YOU ARE COMPLETELY HONEST"
1160 PRINT "BUT OTHERS THINK YOU ARE"
1170 PRINT "FULL OF BULL."
1180 PRINT "A NICE FRIEND WILL VISIT."
1190 GOTO 500
1200 IF D<21 THEN 1110
1210 PRINT "SO, ";N$;", YOU ARE GEMINI"
1220 PRINT "GEMINI IS 'THE TWINS'"
1230 PRINT
1240 PRINT "IT'S HARD FOR YOU TO DECIDE,"
1250 PRINT "YOU OFTEN SPLIT A DECISION."
1260 PRINT "YOU SEE TWO SIDES BUT"
1270 PRINT "FRIENDS FIND YOU DECISIVE."
1280 PRINT "AVOID NEWSPAPER REPORTERS!"
1290 GOTO 500
1300 IF D<21 THEN 1210
1310 PRINT "SO, ";N$;", YOU ARE A CANCER"
1320 PRINT "CANCER IS THE CRAB"
1330 PRINT
1340 PRINT "YOU LIKE TO VENT YOUR"
1350 PRINT "FEELINGS WHEN THINGS"
1360 PRINT "GO WRONG AND FRIENDS"
1370 PRINT "SOMETIMES EXCLUDE YOU."
1380 PRINT "JEWELS WILL BE IN YOUR PATH."
1390 GOTO 500
1400 IF D<23 THEN 1310
1410 PRINT "OKAY, ";N$;", YOU ARE LEO"
1420 PRINT "LEO IS THE LION"
1430 PRINT
1440 PRINT "YOUR ROAR IS WORSE"
1450 PRINT "THAN YOUR BITE."
1460 PRINT "YOUR FRIENDS THINK"
1470 PRINT "YOU ARE A PUSSYCAT."
1480 PRINT "FUR IS IN YOUR FUTURE."
1490 GOTO 500
1500 IF D<23 THEN 1410
1510 PRINT "SO, ";N$;", YOU ARE A VIRGO"
```

```
1520 PRINT "VIRGO IS THE VIRGIN."
1530 PRINT
1540 PRINT "CLEANLINESS IS YOUR VIRTUE."
1550 PRINT "CASUAL ASSOCIATES THINK"
1560 PRINT "YOU ARE TIGHT, BUT THOSE"
1570 PRINT "CLOSE TO YOU KNOW BETTER."
1580 PRINT "AVOID CARS, BARS AND STARS!"
1590 GOTO 500
1600 IF D<24 THEN 1510
1610 PRINT "OKAY, ";N$;", YOU ARE A LIBRA"
1620 PRINT "LIBRA IS 'THE BALANCE'"
1630 PRINT
1640 PRINT "EVERYTHING WORKS OUT FOR"
1650 PRINT "YOU IN THE END BUT PERILS"
1660 PRINT "ALONG THE WAY SOMETIMES"
1670 PRINT "SEEM TO GREAT."
1680 PRINT "YOU WILL FIND THE TRUTH!"
1690 GOTO 500
1700 IF D<24 THEN 1610
1710 PRINT "RIGHT ON, ";N$;" YOU ARE A
     SCORPIO."
1720 PRINT "SCORPIO IS THE SCORPION"
1730 PRINT
1740 PRINT "YOU ARE TRUSTWORTHY, LOYAL,"
1750 PRINT "HELPFUL, FRIENDLY,"
1760 PRINT "COURTEOUS, KIND, OBEDIENT,"
1770 PRINT "CHEERFUL, THRIFTY AND SEXY."
1780 PRINT "YOU WILL WIN!"
1790 GOTO 500
1800 IF D<22 THEN 1710
1810 PRINT "WELL, ";N$;", A SAGITTARIUS"
1820 PRINT "SAGITTARIUS IS THE ARCHER"
1830 PRINT
1840 PRINT "YOU FIRE FROM THE HIP"
1850 PRINT "BUT FRIENDS LIKE YOU ANYWAY"
1860 PRINT "HAPPINESS WILL BE YOURS"
1870 PRINT "BUT WATCH OUT FOR FALSENESS"
1880 GOTO 500
```

Monthly Loan Payment

Here's a fast computation of the monthly payment on a loan. The amount borrowed, the principle, is stored in memory location P. I is the annual interest rate and N is the number of payments. I is converted to a monthly interest rate and then to a decimal in line 50.

Program Listing

```
10 CALL CLEAR
20 INPUT "AMOUNT BORROWED $":P
30 INPUT "ANNUAL INTEREST %":I
40 INPUT "NUMBER OF PAYMENTS ":N
50 I=0.01*(I/12)
60 M=(P*I)/(1-((1+I)^(-N)))
70 PRINT
80 PRINT "MONTHLY PAYMENT IS $";M
90 PRINT
100 PRINT
110 PRINT
120 INPUT "TO DO ANOTHER, PRESS ENTER":KY$
130 GOTO 10
```

Sample Run

```
AMOUNT BORROWED $ 2000
ANNUAL INTEREST %  8
NUMBER OF PAYMENTS  36

MONTHLY PAYMENT IS $ 62.67273092




AMOUNT BORROWED $ 1000
ANNUAL INTEREST %  14
NUMBER OF PAYMENTS  48

MONTHLY PAYMENT IS $ 27.32647649
```

Number Of Days In A Month

Here's a cute teacher for your elementary-age kids. This program displays the name of a month and asks how many days in that month. If the correct number of days is entered, the computer says "correct." If an incorrect number of days is entered, the computer says "wrong." In either case, the correct answer is displayed. The educational game can go on forever if needed.

We've put DATA in lines 20 to 130 and questions about that data in lines 230 and 210. You can change the data to whatever you like and the same for the questions.

Remember that you must have only two items in each DATA line. The machine will present the first of the two items in line 210 and looks for the second item in response to the question in line 230.

For example, in our sample program, we gave the computer the names of the 12 months of the year and the number of days in each month. Note that a comma must separate the two items in a DATA line.

The computer prints the name of a month, randomly selected, and asks how many days are in that month. You answer. It reports whether or not you answered correctly and displays the correct answer. Then it randomly selects another month and starts over.

You may add additional DATA lines if your quiz needs to be longer. Remember that DATA lines can be located anywhere in a program so you could add more on the end starting at line 320, if you like.

Program Listing

```
10 CALL CLEAR
15 RANDOMIZE
20 DATA JANUARY,31
30 DATA FEBRUARY,28
40 DATA MARCH,31
50 DATA APRIL,30
60 DATA MAY,31
70 DATA JUNE,30
80 DATA JULY,31
90 DATA AUGUST,31
```

```
100 DATA SEPTEMBER,30
110 DATA OCTOBER,31
120 DATA NOVEMBER,30
130 DATA DECEMBER,31
140 R=INT(25*RND)
150 IF INT(R/2)=(R/2)THEN 170
160 GOTO 180
170 R=R-1
180 FOR L=1 TO R
190 READ S$
200 NEXT L
210 PRINT "MONTH IS ";S$
220 READ C$
230 INPUT "HOW MANY DAYS?":D$
240 IF D$=C$ THEN 270
250 PRINT "WRONG"
260 GOTO 280
270 PRINT "RIGHT"
280 PRINT "NUMBER OF DAYS IS ";C$
290 RESTORE
300 PRINT
310 GOTO 140
```

Sample Run

```
MONTH IS DECEMBER
HOW MANY DAYS? 31
RIGHT
NUMBER OF DAYS IS 31

MONTH IS OCTOBER
HOW MANY DAYS? 31
RIGHT
NUMBER OF DAYS IS 31

MONTH IS JULY
HOW MANY DAYS? 31
RIGHT
NUMBER OF DAYS IS 31
```

Poetrywriter™

Well, we said it could do *anything*! All you have to do is explain to your computer about adjectives, nouns, verbs and adverbs. Give it a nice little vocabulary. And off it goes, writing poetry.

The vocabulary is held as DATA in lines 20 to 200. The relationship of the words in each of those program lines is important if you want the computer to make sense with proper syntax.

Each DATA line has seven items (after the BASIC word DATA). The seventh "word" actually is a phrase as we use it but is treated as one unit. The seven items are separated by commas.

We use the first English word in the DATA line for transitions. The second and third English words are adjectives.

The fourth word is a plural noun. The fifth word is a verb. The sixth word is an adverb. And the seventh item is a colorful phrase. It could just as well be a single word.

The computer randomly selects one of each of the seven types of English words and puts them together to form sentences.

Random number generators are in lines 300, 400, 500, 600, 700, 800, and 900. Punctuation and print-out order is determined in lines 1000 to 1100.

The computer will write poems all day until you press its BREAK key.

Program Listing

```
10 CALL CLEAR
15 RANDOMIZE
20 DATA THE,BIG,BLUE,MARBLES,RUN,
   SMOOTHLY,IN THE SAND
30 DATA WHILE,JOLLY,GREEN,GIANTS,EAT,
   HEARTILY,ON THE HILL
40 DATA AND,FRIENDLY,OLD,BOYS,WEAR,
   WELL,AS THEY AGE
50 DATA OR,HARD,PLASTIC,BUTTONS,LAST,
   TOUGHLY,FOREVER
```

```
 60 DATA WHEN,HAIRY,TINY,DOGS,PASS,
    RUGGEDLY,IN THE NIGHT
 70 DATA FROM,WEALTHY,RED,BAGS,TALK,
    HAPPILY,FROM THE VALLEY
 80 DATA FOR,LIVELY,MEAN,FOLKS,PLOW,
    NICELY,ABOVE THE CLOUDS
 90 DATA THE,PRETTY,TIMELY,LOVERS,FLY,
    LOOSELY,IN THE GROUND
100 DATA MEANWHILE,SAD,YOUNG,CATS,GRIND,
    CONCRETELY,BEHIND THE BARN
110 DATA FROM,TIRED,POOR,DRINKERS,FLASH,
    BRIGHTLY,IN THE PAN
120 DATA ABOUT,TIGHT,BALD,WIVES,PLAY,
    NOISELY,BEYOND THE PALE
130 DATA THE,FOLDED,GLOWING,FARMERS,
    SHINE,MERRILY,TOWARD OUR LIVES
140 DATA AND,ROUGH,DARK,HENCHMEN,TRYST,
    SWEETLY,NEAR A TREE
150 DATA AS,TIMELY,ROUND,PRIESTS,FOLLOW,
    BLINDLY,DOWN THE TUBES
160 DATA WHILE,CRUNCHY,BULKY,STATUES,
    LIFT,WETLY,IN THE BOX
170 DATA AND,GOLDEN,SILVERY,BODIES,TURN,
    FREELY,IN THE WIND
180 DATA WHILE,NAKED,CARVED,FLOWERS,GLOW,
    SMARTLY,FROM A MOUNTAIN
190 DATA WHERE,SPARKLING,LOUD,MEN,FIGHT,
    WHOLEHEARTEDLY,TO THE DEATH
200 DATA AND,FRESH,NEW,ANCIENTS,HUMANIZE,
    BRAZENLY,FOR THE REST

300 GOSUB 1200
330 FOR L=1 TO R
340 READ V$
350 NEXT L
360 RESTORE
400 GOSUB 1200
430 FOR L=1 TO R-1
440 READ W$
450 NEXT L
460 RESTORE
```

```
500 GOSUB 1200
530 FOR L=1 TO R-2
540 READ X$
550 NEXT L
560 RESTORE
600 GOSUB 1200
630 FOR L=1 TO R-3
640 READ Y$
650 NEXT L
660 RESTORE
700 GOSUB 1200
730 FOR L=1 TO R-4
740 READ Z$
750 NEXT L
760 RESTORE
800 GOSUB 1200
830 FOR L=1 TO R-5
840 READ A$
850 NEXT L
860 RESTORE
900 GOSUB 1200
930 FOR L=1 TO R-6
940 READ B$
950 NEXT L
960 RESTORE
1000 D=D+1
1010 IF INT(D/2)=(D/2)THEN 1030
1020 PRINT A$;" ";Z$;" ";Y$
1025 GOTO 1040
1030 PRINT B$;" ";A$;" ";Z$;" ";Y$
1040 IF INT(D/2)=(D/2)THEN 1060
1050 PRINT X$;" ";W$;" ";V$;","
1055 GOTO 1070
1060 PRINT X$;" ";W$;" ";V$;"."
1070 IF INT(D/2)=(D/2)THEN 1085
1080 GOTO 1090
1085 PRINT
1090 IF D<12 THEN 300
1100 D=0
1110 PRINT
1120 PRINT
1130 GOTO 300
```

```
1200 R=INT(133*RND)
1210 IF R<7 THEN 1200
1220 IF INT(R/7)<>(R/7)THEN 1200
1230 RETURN
```

Program Listing

```
1 REM *****POETRYWRITER (tm)
2 REM *****USE THIS VERSION OF THE
  PROGRAM IF YOU HAVE A PRINTER.
3 REM *****IT WILL GIVE YOU A HARDCOPY
  PRINTOUT OF THE POEMS AS IN OUR
  SAMPLE RUN.
4 REM ***********************************
10 CALL CLEAR
15 RANDOMIZE
20 DATA THE,BIG,BLUE,MARBLES,RUN,
   SMOOTHLY,IN THE SAND
30 DATA WHILE,JOLLY,GREEN,GIANTS,EAT,
   HEARTILY,ON THE HILL
40 DATA AND,FRIENDLY,OLD,BOYS,WEAR,WELL,
   AS THEY AGE
50 DATA OR,HARD,PLASTIC,BUTTONS,LAST,
   TOUGHLY,FOREVER
60 DATA WHEN,HAIRY,TINY,DOGS,PASS,
   RUGGEDLY,IN THE NIGHT
70 DATA FROM,WEALTHY,RED,BAGS,TALK,
   HAPPILY,FROM THE VALLEY
80 DATA FOR,LIVELY,MEAN,FOLKS,PLOW,
   NICELY,ABOVE THE CLOUDS
90 DATA THE,PRETTY,TIMELY,LOVERS,FLY,
   LOOSELY,IN THE GROUND
100 DATA MEANWHILE,SAD,YOUNG,CATS,GRIND,
    CONCRETELY,BEHIND THE BARN
110 DATA FROM,TIRED,POOR,DRINKERS,FLASH,
    BRIGHTLY,IN THE PAN
120 DATA ABOUT,TIGHT,BALD,WIVES,PLAY,
    NOISELY,BEYOND THE PALE
130 DATA THE,FOLDED,GLOWING,FARMERS,
    SHINE,MERRILY,TOWARD OUR LIVES
```

```
140 DATA AND,ROUGH,DARK,HENCHMEN,TRYST,
    SWEETLY,NEAR A TREE
150 DATA AS,TIMELY,ROUND,PRIESTS,FOLLOW,
    BLINDLY,DOWN THE TUBES
160 DATA WHILE,CRUNCHY,BULKY,STATUES,
    LIFT,WETLY,IN THE BOX
170 DATA AND,GOLDEN,SILVERY,BODIES,TURN,
    FREELY,IN THE WIND
180 DATA WHILE,NAKED,CARVED,FLOWERS,GLOW,
    SMARTLY,FROM A MOUNTAIN
190 DATA WHERE,SPARKLING,LOUD,MEN,FIGHT,
    WHOLEHEARTEDLY,TO THE DEATH
200 DATA AND,FRESH,NEW,ANCIENTS,HUMANIZE,
    BRAZENLY,FOR THE REST
250 OPEN #1:"RS232"
300 GOSUB 1200
330 FOR L=1 TO R
340 READ V$
350 NEXT L
360 RESTORE
400 GOSUB 1200
430 FOR L=1 TO R-1
440 READ W$
450 NEXT L
460 RESTORE
500 GOSUB 1200
530 FOR L=1 TO R-2'
540 READ X$
550 NEXT L
560 RESTORE
600 GOSUB 1200
630 FOR L=1 TO R-3
640 READ Y$
650 NEXT L
660 RESTORE
700 GOSUB 1200
730 FOR L=1 TO R-4
740 READ Z$
750 NEXT L
760 RESTORE
800 GOSUB 1200
```

```
830 FOR L=1 TO R-5
840 READ A$
850 NEXT L
860 RESTORE
900 GOSUB 1200
930 FOR L=1 TO R-6
940 READ B$
950 NEXT L
960 RESTORE
1000 D=D+1
1010 IF INT(D/2)=(D/2)THEN 1030
1020 PRINT #1:A$;" ";Z$;" ";Y$
1025 GOTO 1040
1030 PRINT #1:B$;" ";A$;" ";Z$;" ";Y$
1040 IF INT(D/2)=(D/2)THEN 1060
1050 PRINT #1:X$;" ";W$;" ";V$;","
1055 GOTO 1070
1060 PRINT #1:X$;" ";W$;" ";V$;"."
1070 IF INT(D/2)=(D/2)THEN 1085
1080 GOTO 1090
1085 PRINT #1
1090 IF D<12 THEN 300
1100 D=0
1110 PRINT #1
1120 PRINT #1
1130 GOTO 300
1200 R=INT(133*RND)
1210 IF R<7 THEN 1200
1220 IF INT(R/7)<>(R/7)THEN 1200
1230 RETURN
```

Sample Run

```
GOLDEN GREEN PRIESTS
WEAR TOUGHLY IN THE SAND,
WHERE WEALTHY LOUD BAGS
LAST MERRILY TOWARD OUR LIVES.

FRIENDLY TINY DRINKERS
PASS WHOLEHEARTEDLY FROM A MOUNTAIN,
AS ROUGH GLOWING LOVERS
GRIND HEARTILY IN THE WIND.
```

HARD BLUE BUTTONS
WEAR BLINDLY ON THE HILL,
WHEN ROUGH POOR CATS
FLY CONCRETELY BEHIND THE BARN.

TIMELY BALD CATS
TALK RUGGEDLY TOWARD OUR LIVES,
FROM FOLDED GREEN PRIESTS
FLASH FREELY AS THEY AGE.

SPARKLING YOUNG FLOWERS
LAST SMOOTHLY TO THE DEATH,
MEANWHILE GOLDEN CARVED BAGS
FLY SMARTLY FOREVER.

HARD BLUE MARBLES
PLAY CONCRETELY ABOVE THE CLOUDS,
WHILE BIG BALD BOYS
EAT BLINDLY IN THE NIGHT.

Sample Run

WEALTHY LOUD MEN
FOLLOW SMOOTHLY FOREVER,
FROM GOLDEN POOR BAGS
EAT SWEETLY BEYOND THE PALE.

WEALTHY DARK BODIES
PLOW SMOOTHLY BEHIND THE BARN,
WHERE PRETTY SILVERY BOYS
WEAR WELL TO THE DEATH.

GOLDEN CARVED CATS
FLY FREELY TO THE DEATH,
WHILE LIVELY GLOWING MARBLES
GLOW MERRILY TOWARD OUR LIVES.

LIVELY TIMELY FOLKS
TRYST WELL FROM A MOUNTAIN,
THE BIG OLD CATS
FLY FREELY IN THE WIND.

High/Low Bowling Score

Suppose you bowl with a group of friends, each with a different score or set of scores? This program accepts their names and scores and sorts out the persons with the highest and the lowest bowling scores.

To complete data entry, simply press ENTER without data. That prompts your computer, via lines 140 and 150, to print the lowest score and the highest score.

Naturally, this kind of sorting could be applied to any game with ranges of scores among different players.

Program Listing

```
10 CALL CLEAR
20 X=0
30 CALL SOUND(1,1000,15)
40 INPUT "NAME: ":N$
50 IF N$="" THEN 120
60 INPUT "SCORE: ":S
70 X=X+1
80 IF X=1 THEN 300
90 IF S<LS THEN 400
100 IF S>HS THEN 500
110 GOTO 40
120 PRINT
125 PRINT
130 CALL SOUND(1,1000,15)
140 PRINT "LOWEST SCORE:   ";LS;" ";LN$
150 PRINT "HIGHEST SCORE: ";HS;" ";HN$
160 PRINT
170 PRINT
180 PRINT
190 INPUT "TO DO MORE, PRESS ENTER":KY$
200 LS=0
210 HS=0
220 GOTO 10
300 LS=S
310 LN$=N$
320 HS=S
330 HN$=N$
```

```
340 GOTO 110
400 LS=S
410 LN$=N$
420 GOTO 110
500 HS=S
510 HN$=N$
520 GOTO 110
```

Sample Run

```
NAME: EDWARD
SCORE:  55
NAME: JAMES
SCORE:  66
NAME: MARTHA
SCORE:  77
NAME: JULES
SCORE:  22
NAME:


LOWEST SCORE:    22   JULES
HIGHEST SCORE:   77   MARTHA



TO DO MORE, PRESS ENTER
NAME: MIKE
SCORE:  654
NAME: PAT
SCORE:  456
NAME: LOU
SCORE:  123
NAME: RON
SCORE:  999
NAME:


LOWEST SCORE:    123   LOU
HIGHEST SCORE:   999   RON
```

Random Number Quality Checker

Ever wonder just how unintentional, haphazard, or unrelated your random numbers are? This program reinforces your confidence in the pseudorandom number generator in the computer.

It causes the machine to generate 100 numbers between zero and 100 and reports how many are above 49 and how many are below 50.

Just for fun, we've thrown in an executive decision maker. That is, the board of directors voted 47 yes, 53 no. Can you imagine it?

Program Listing

```
10 CALL CLEAR
20 X=0
30 FOR L=1 TO 100
40 X=INT(101*RND)
50 IF X<50 THEN 200
60 IF X>49 THEN 300
70 NEXT L
80 PRINT "YES",Y
90 PRINT "NO",N
100 PRINT
110 Y=0
120 N=0
130 GOTO 20
200 Y=Y+1
210 GOTO 70
300 N=N+1
310 GOTO 70
```

Sample Run

```
YES          43
NO           57

YES          49
NO           51
```

Super Slot-O

Oh, those evil slot machines! They're just popping up everywhere. Even inside my TI Computer.

As with all the programs used as examples in this book, simply type this one in and RUN it. The computer will display, on your video screen, the name of this program and some simple instructions.

Like any good slot machine, when you pull the handle it displays some objects. If you get no two alike, you lose. If you get two alike among the three objects, you win small. If all three are the same, you win big.

To simulate pulling the slot machine's lever arm, press the ENTER key on the keyboard.

One difference in our Slot-O game, the display is entirely at random. No one pushes a secret button under the table to make certain items pop up.

Get out your funny-money from that old Monopoly game, gather up your friends, and let's have some fun.

Program Listing

```
10 CALL CLEAR
20 GOSUB 500
30 PRINT
40 PRINT
50 PRINT
60 GOSUB 200
70 PRINT "***** ***** ***** *****"
80 PRINT "* ";A$;" * * ";B$;" * * "
   ;C$;" * * ";D$;" *"
90 PRINT "***** ***** ***** *****"
100 PRINT
105 PRINT
110 PRINT "TO PULL THE LEVER,"
120 INPUT "PRESS ENTER":KY$
130 GOTO 10
200 GOSUB 400
210 A$=CHR$(X)
220 GOSUB 400
230 B$=CHR$(X)
240 GOSUB 400
```

```
250 C$=CHR$(X)
260 GOSUB 400
270 D$=CHR$(X)
280 GOSUB 400
400 R=INT(5*RND)
410 IF R<1 THEN 400
420 IF R=1 THEN 800
430 IF R=2 THEN 900
440 IF R=3 THEN 1000
450 IF R=4 THEN 1100
460 RETURN
500 PRINT "**********************"
510 PRINT "* SUPER T.I. SLOT-O *"
520 PRINT "**********************"
530 RETURN
800 X=35
810 GOTO 460
900 X=36
910 GOTO 460
1000 X=37
1010 GOTO 460
1100 X=38
1110 GOTO 460
```

Sample Run

```
**********************
* SUPER T.I. SLOT-O *
**********************


***** ***** ***** *****
* $ * * # * * $ * * # *
***** ***** ***** *****


TO PULL THE LEVER,
PRESS ENTER
```

```
*********************
* SUPER T.I. SLOT-O *
*********************

***** ***** ***** *****
* # * * $ * * % * * & *
***** ***** ***** *****


TO PULL THE LEVER,
PRESS ENTER
```

Savings Quickie

Want a quick idea of how much your savings account will grow over the years? This program is fast to load and speedy to run.

The computer will ask for initial savings balance, annual interest percentage rate, and number of years. In return, it computes compound interest and displays the savings balance at the end of each year in a handy list.

Program Listing

```
10 CALL CLEAR
20 B=0
30 I=0
40 Y=0
50 Z=0
60 INPUT "PRESENT SAVINGS BALANCE: $":B
70 INPUT "INTEREST RATE PERCENT: ":I
80 INPUT "NUMBER OF YEARS: ":Y
90 FOR L=1 TO Y
100 Z=Z+I*(Z+B)/100
110 PRINT L,Z+B
120 NEXT L
130 FOR A=1 TO 4
140 PRINT
150 NEXT A
160 INPUT "TO DO ANOTHER, PRESS ENTER":KY$
170 GOTO 10
```

Sample Run

```
PRESENT SAVINGS BALANCE: $ 652
INTEREST RATE PERCENT:   8
NUMBER OF YEARS:   11
    1             704.16
    2             760.4928
    3             821.332224
    4             887.0388019
    5             958.0019061
    6             1034.642059
    7             1117.413423
    8             1206.806497
    9             1303.351017
   10             1407.619098
   11             1520.228626


TO DO ANOTHER, PRESS ENTER

PRESENT SAVINGS BALANCE: $ 1000
INTEREST RATE PERCENT:   7.5
NUMBER OF YEARS:   5
    1             1075
    2             1155.625
    3             1242.296875
    4             1335.469141
    5             1435.629326

TO DO ANOTHER, PRESS ENTER

PRESENT SAVINGS BALANCE: $ 300
INTEREST RATE PERCENT:   6
NUMBER OF YEARS:   3
    1             318
    2             337.08
    3             357.3048


TO DO ANOTHER, PRESS ENTER
```

Draw Straws

Here's one of man's oldest decision makers. Several straws are broken off to the same length except for one extra-short straw. The length of all straws is concealed and each person draws a straw. The person drawing the shortest straw "wins." That is, he is selected by the luck of the draw.

Now, your computer can provide a fast and easy drawing where no straws are available. It does all the work for you by assigning electronic straws randomly to each person. Those straws are numbers. The shortest straw, or lowest number, "wins."

Program Listing

```
10 CALL CLEAR
20 B=0
30 C=0
40 D=0
50 L=0
60 X=0
70 GOSUB 500
80 PRINT
90 PRINT "DRAW STRAWS"
100 GOSUB 500
110 PRINT
120 PRINT
130 INPUT "PLAYER NO. 1: ":B$
140 INPUT "PLAYER NO. 2: ":C$
150 INPUT "PLAYER NO. 3: ":D$
160 GOSUB 540
170 B=X
180 L=B
190 GOSUB 540
200 C=X
210 IF C<L THEN 230
220 GOTO 240
230 L=C
240 GOSUB 540
250 D=X
```

```
260 IF D<L THEN 280
270 GOTO 290
280 L=D
290 PRINT
300 PRINT
310 PRINT B$;": ";B;
320 IF L=B THEN 350
330 PRINT
340 GOTO 360
350 PRINT " <<<<<"
360 PRINT C$;": ";C;
370 IF L=C THEN 400
380 PRINT
390 GOTO 410
400 PRINT " <<<<<"
410 PRINT D$;": ";D;
420 IF L=D THEN 450
430 PRINT
440 GOTO 460
450 PRINT " <<<<<"
460 PRINT
470 PRINT
480 INPUT "FOR MORE, PRESS ENTER":KY$
490 GOTO 10
500 FOR L=1 TO 11
510 PRINT "*";
520 NEXT L
530 RETURN
540 X=INT(100*RND)
550 RETURN
```

Funny similes

Give these newfangled gadgets an inch and they'll take a mile. In the case of the computer, give it some tacky retorts and it will spew out an endless string of dumb remarks.

The fun is in having the computer randomly select various words and combine them to make silly sayings.

The random number is used to match the words into similes.

Program Listing

```
10 RANDOMIZE
20 CALL CLEAR
30 DATA SHORT,TALL,FAT,LEAN,CLEAN
40 DATA DIRTY,GOOD,BAD,HAPPY,SAD
50 DATA GREEN,RED,YELLOW,BLUE,UGLY
60 DATA PRETTY,SHARP,DULL,TACKY,NATTY
70 DATA STRONG,WEAK,MEAN,NICE,DUMB
80 DATA GNOME,TREE,PIG,BOX,CLOCK
90 DATA TURKEY,GOLD,APPLE,DOG,ROOKIE
100 DATA BEET,BIRD,SKY,SIN,PEACH
110 DATA TACK,RAZOR,PIN,PLUG,BULL
120 DATA WORM,LION,LAMB,PUPPY,OX
130 PRINT "WHOM ARE WE DESCRIBING"
140 INPUT B$
150 PRINT
160 T=INT(26*RND)
170 IF T<1 THEN 160
180 IF T>25 THEN 160
190 FOR L=1 TO T
200 READ D$
210 NEXT L
220 RESTORE
230 T=INT(51*RND)
240 IF T<26 THEN 230
250 IF T>50 THEN 230
260 FOR L=1 TO T
270 READ E$
280 NEXT L
290 RESTORE
300 CALL SOUND(1,1000,19)
310 PRINT B$;" IS ";D$;" AS A ";E$
320 FOR L=1 TO 8
330 PRINT
340 NEXT L
350 INPUT "FOR ANOTHER, PRESS ENTER":KY$
360 GOTO 20
```

Birthstones

What's your Mother's birthstone? You'd better know! If not, take this little quiz a few times until you get all 12 months memorized.

The computer presents the name of a month. You type in the name of the birthstone (correctly spelled) for that month.

Program Listing

```
10 CALL CLEAR
15 RANDOMIZE
20 DATA JANUARY,GARNET
30 DATA FEBRUARY,AMETHYST
40 DATA MARCH,AQUAMARINE
50 DATA APRIL,DIAMOND
60 DATA MAY,EMERALD
70 DATA JUNE,PEARL
80 DATA JULY,RUBY
90 DATA AUGUST,PERIDOT
100 DATA SEPTEMBER,SAPPHIRE
110 DATA OCTOBER,OPAL
120 DATA NOVEMBER,TOPAZ
130 DATA DECEMBER,TURQUOISE
140 PRINT "***************"
150 PRINT "* BIRTHSTONES *"
160 PRINT "***************"
170 PRINT
180 PRINT "HOW MANY MONTHS DO YOU KNOW?"
190 FOR Q=1 TO 11
200 PRINT
210 NEXT Q
220 PRINT "PRESS ANY KEY TO START"
230 CALL KEY(0,Z,X)
240 IF X=0 THEN 230
250 CALL CLEAR
260 R=INT(25*RND)
270 IF R<1 THEN 260
280 IF INT(R/2)=(R/2)THEN 300
290 GOTO 310
300 R=R-1
```

```
310 FOR L=1 TO R
320 READ S$
330 NEXT L
340 PRINT
350 PRINT
360 PRINT "WHAT IS THE BIRTHSTONE"
370 PRINT "FOR ";S$
380 READ C$
390 INPUT D$
400 PRINT
410 IF D$=C$ THEN 440
420 PRINT "WRONG"
430 GOTO 450
440 PRINT "RIGHT !"
450 PRINT "THE BIRTHSTONE FOR ";S$
460 PRINT "IS THE ";C$
470 RESTORE
480 FOR Q=1 TO 10
490 PRINT
500 NEXT Q
510 GOTO 260
```

Sample Run

```
***************
* BIRTHSTONES *
***************
HOW MANY MONTHS DO YOU KNOW?
PRESS ANY KEY TO START
WHAT IS THE BIRTHSTONE
FOR JULY?
RUBY
RIGHT !
THE BIRTHSTONE FOR JULY
IS THE RUBY

WHAT IS THE BIRTHSTONE
FOR MAY?
EMERALD
RIGHT !
THE BIRTHSTONE FOR MAY
IS THE EMERALD
```

```
=GHIJKLMNOPQRSTUVWXYZ[\]^_`abcdefghi jk
GHIJKLMNOPQRSTUVWXYZ[\]^_`abcdefghi jkl
HIJKLMNOPQRSTUVWXYZ[\]^_`abcdefghi jklm
IJKLMNOPQRSTUVWXYZ[\]^_`abcdefghi jklmn
JKLMNOPQRSTUVWXYZ[\]^_`abcdefghi jklmno
KLMNOPQRSTUVWXYZ[\]^_`abcdefghi jklmnop
LMNOPQRSTUVWXYZ[\]^_`abcdefghi jklmnopq
MNOPQRSTUVWXYZ[\]^_`abcdefghi jklmnopqr
NOPQRSTUVWXYZ[\]^_`abcdefghi jklmnopqrs
OPQRSTUVWXYZ[\]^_`abcdefghi jklmnopqrst
PQRSTUVWXYZ[\]^_`abcdefghi jklmnopqrstu
QRSTUVWXYZ[\]^_`abcdefghi jklmnopqrstuv
RSTUVWXYZ[\]^_`abcdefghi jklmnopqrstuvw
STUVWXYZ[\]^_`abcdefghi jklmnopqrstuvwx
TUVWXYZ[\]^_`abcdefghi jklmnopqrstuvwxy
UVWXYZ[\]^_`abcdefghi jklmnopqrstuvwxyz
VWXYZ[\]^_`abcdefghi jklmnopqrstuvwxyz {
WXYZ[\]^_`abcdefghi jklmnopqrstuvwxyz {|
XYZ[\]^_`abcdefghi jklmnopqrstuvwxyz {|}
YZ[\]^_`abcdefghi jklmnopqrstuvwxyz {|}~
Z[\]^_`abcdefghi jklmnopqrstuvwxyz {|}~
[\]^_`abcdefghi jklmnopqrstuvwxyz {|}~ !
\]^_`abcdefghi jklmnopqrstuvwxyz {|}~ !"
]^_`abcdefghi jklmnopqrstuvwxyz {|}~ !"#
^_`abcdefghi jklmnopqrstuvwxyz {|}~ !"#$
_`abcdefghi jklmnopqrstuvwxyz {|}~ !"#$%
`abcdefghi jklmnopqrstuvwxyz {|}~ !"#$%&
abcdefghi jklmnopqrstuvwxyz {|}~ !"#$%&'
bcdefghi jklmnopqrstuvwxyz {|}~ !"#$%&'(
cdefghi jklmnopqrstuvwxyz {|}~ !"#$%&'()
defghi jklmnopqrstuvwxyz {|}~ !"#$%&'()*
efghi jklmnopqrstuvwxyz {|}~ !"#$%&'()*+
fghi jklmnopqrstuvwxyz {|}~ !"#$%&'()*+,
ghi jklmnopqrstuvwxyz {|}~ !"#$%&'()*+,-
hi jklmnopqrstuvwxyz {|}~ !"#$%&'()*+,-.
i jklmnopqrstuvwxyz {|}~ !"#$%&'()*+,-./
jklmnopqrstuvwxyz {|}~ !"#$%&'()*+,-./0
klmnopqrstuvwxyz {|}~ !"#$%&'()*+,-./01
lmnopqrstuvwxyz {|}~ !"#$%&'()*+,-./012
mnopqrstuvwxyz {|}~ !"#$%&'()*+,-./0123
nopqrstuvwxyz {|}~ !"#$%&'()*+,-./01234
opqrstuvwxyz {|}~ !"#$%&'()*+,-./012345
```

Programs
for the classroom

Foreign Capitals

Here's a learning quiz we'll bet you haven't seen anywhere else. This program tests your knowledge of foreign countries. The more you play, the more you learn!

You must tell the computer the correct name of the capital of the country it presents. And you must spell the name of that city correctly.

What is the capital of Egypt, Poland, Turkey, New Zealand, Bolivia or Afghanistan? It can be very tough!

Want to change to different countries? Change the DATA lines 20 to 540. Be sure to put a comma between country and capital in each DATA line.

Program Listing

```
10 RANDOMIZE
15 CALL CLEAR
20 DATA AFGHANISTAN,KABUL
30 DATA ALBANIA,TIRANA
40 DATA ALGERIA,ALGIERS
50 DATA ARGENTINA,BUENOS AIRES
60 DATA AUSTRALIA,CANBERRA
70 DATA AUSTRIA,VIENNA
80 DATA BAHRAIN,MANAMA
90 DATA BANGLADESH,DACCA
100 DATA BELGIUM,BRUSSELS
110 DATA BOLIVIA,LA PAZ
120 DATA BRAZIL,BRASILIA
130 DATA BULGARIA,SOFIA
140 DATA BURMA,RANGOON
150 DATA CHILE,SANTIAGO
160 DATA COLOMBIA,BOGOTA
170 DATA CUBA,HAVANA
180 DATA CZECHOSLOVAKIA,PRAGUE
190 DATA DENMARK,COPENHAGEN
200 DATA EGYPT,CAIRO
210 DATA FINLAND,HELSINKI
220 DATA FRANCE,PARIS
230 DATA GERMANY EAST,EAST BERLIN
```

```
240 DATA GERMANY WEST,BONN
250 DATA GREECE,ATHENS
260 DATA HAITI,PORT-AU-PRINCE
270 DATA HUNGARY,BUDAPEST
280 DATA ICELAND,REYKJAVIK
290 DATA INDIA,NEW DELHI
300 DATA IRAN,TEHRAN
310 DATA ITALY,ROME
320 DATA JAPAN,TOKYO
330 DATA KUWAIT,KUWAIT
340 DATA LIBYA,TRIPOLI
350 DATA MEXICO,MEXICO CITY
360 DATA NEPAL,KATHMANDU
370 DATA NEW ZEALAND,WELLINGTON
380 DATA NORWAY,OSLO
390 DATA OMAN,MUSCAT
400 DATA PERU,LIMA
410 DATA POLAND,WARSAW
420 DATA QATAR,DOHA
430 DATA ROMANIA,BUCHAREST
440 DATA SPAIN,MADRID
450 DATA SUDAN,KHARTOUM
460 DATA SWEDEN,STOCKHOLM
470 DATA SWITZERLAND,BERN
480 DATA TURKEY,ANKARA
490 DATA U.S.S.R.,MOSCOW
500 DATA UNITED KINGDOM,LONDON
510 DATA VENEZUELA,CARACAS
520 DATA YUGOSLAVIA,BELGRADE
530 DATA ZAIRE,KINSHASA
540 DATA ZAMBIA,LUSAKA
550 PRINT "*****FOREIGN CAPITALS*****"
560 R=INT(106*RND)
570 IF R<1 THEN 560
580 IF INT(R/2)=(R/2)THEN 600
590 GOTO 610
600 R=R-1
610 FOR L=1 TO R
620 READ S$
630 NEXT L
640 PRINT
650 PRINT
```

```
660 PRINT "COUNTRY: ";S$
670 READ C$
680 INPUT "WHAT IS THE CAPITAL ":D$
690 IF D$=C$ THEN 710
700 GOTO 730
710 PRINT "RIGHT"
720 GOTO 740
730 PRINT "WRONG"
740 PRINT "CAPITAL OF ";S$;" IS ";C$
750 RESTORE
760 PRINT
770 PRINT
780 GOTO 560
```

Areas

Circle. Ellipse. Parabola. Sphere. Square. Rectangle. Triangle. Name your shape. This program will compute its area. Surface area in the case of the sphere. Answer the computer's questions and it will give you the answer you need, in square units of measure. If you use inches, the answer will be in square inches. Put in yards and get square yards. Meters, get square meters. Please don't mix units in any one computation.

Program Listing

```
10 CALL CLEAR
20 INPUT "SHAPE: ":S$
30 IF S$="CIRCLE" THEN 100
40 IF S$="ELLIPSE" THEN 200
50 IF S$="PARABOLA" THEN 300
60 IF S$="SPHERE" THEN 400
70 IF S$="SQUARE" THEN 500
80 IF S$="RECTANGLE" THEN 500
90 IF S$="TRIANGLE" THEN 600
95 GOTO 20
100 INPUT "RADIUS = ":R
110 A=3.141592654*(R^2)
120 GOTO 700
```

```
200 INPUT "MAJOR AXIS = ":J
210 INPUT "MINOR AXIS = ":N
220 A=0.7854*J*N
230 GOTO 700
300 INPUT "BASE = ":B
310 INPUT "HEIGHTH = ":H
320 A=(2/3)*(B*H)
330 GOTO 700
400 INPUT "RADIUS = ":R
410 A=3.141592654*4*(R^2)
420 GOTO 700
500 INPUT "LENGTH = ":L
510 IF S$="SQUARE" THEN 550
520 INPUT "WIDTH = ":W
530 A=L*W
540 GOTO 700
550 A=L*L
560 GOTO 700
600 INPUT "BASE = ":B
610 INPUT "HEIGHTH = ":H
620 A=0.5*B*H
700 PRINT
720 PRINT "AREA = ";A
730 PRINT
740 PRINT
750 R=0
760 J=0
770 N=0
780 B=0
790 H=0
800 L=0
810 W=0
820 GOTO 20
```

Sample Run

```
SHAPE: TRIANGLE
BASE =  55
HEIGHTH =  22

AREA =  605
```

```
SHAPE: ELLIPSE
MAJOR AXIS =   19
MINOR AXIS =   14

AREA =   208.9164

SHAPE: CIRCLE
RADIUS =   13

AREA =   530.9291585

SHAPE: PARABOLA
BASE =   18
HEIGHTH =   37

AREA =   444

SHAPE: SQUARE
LENGTH =   44

AREA =   1936

SHAPE: SPHERE
RADIUS =   13

AREA =   2123.716634

SHAPE: RECTANGLE
LENGTH =   22
WIDTH =   55

AREA =   1210
```

Photography: Flash Exposure

Use your computer to help take better pictures!
The most important factor in pictures shot with flash is
the distance from your flash to the subject. Subjects

which are close to you will receive a lot of light while subjects farther away will receive less light.

Check your data sheet for the film you are using. Look
for the film guide number. Next, make an estimate of the
distance in feet from the flash to your subject.

This program determines the proper f/stop setting for
your camera. By the way, if the computer tells you to use
an f/stop setting between two f/numbers available on your
camera, set your lens opening at the nearest f/number or
halfway between the two, whichever is closest.

For example, suppose your film has a guide number of
80 and you estimate the flash-to-subject distance at 10
feet. Use f/8 on your lens.

Program Listing

```
10 CALL CLEAR
20 PRINT "PHOTOGRAPHY: FLASH EXPOSURE"
30 PRINT "****************************"
40 PRINT
50 INPUT "WHAT IS FILM GUIDE NUMBER ":G
60 INPUT "WHAT IS THE FLASH-TO-SUBJECT
   DISTANCE ":D
100 F=G/D
110 CALL SOUND(1,1000,20)
120 CALL CLEAR
130 PRINT "GUIDE NUMBER: ";G
140 PRINT "DISTANCE:      ";D
150 PRINT "SHOOT AT:      F/";F
200 FOR L=1 TO 6
210 PRINT
220 NEXT L
230 INPUT "FOR MORE, PRESS ENTER":KY$
240 GOTO 10
```

Sample Run

```
PHOTOGRAPHY: FLASH EXPOSURE
****************************

WHAT IS FILM GUIDE NUMBER   80
WHAT IS THE FLASH-TO-SUBJECT DISTANCE  10
```

```
GUIDE NUMBER:    80
DISTANCE:        10
SHOOT AT:        F/ 8


FOR MORE, PRESS ENTER

PHOTOGRAPHY: FLASH EXPOSURE
******************************

WHAT IS FILM GUIDE NUMBER    50
WHAT IS THE FLASH-TO-SUBJECT DISTANCE    5
GUIDE NUMBER:    50
DISTANCE:        5
SHOOT AT:        F/ 10


FOR MORE, PRESS ENTER
```

Photography: Close Ups

For copying and other close-up work with your camera, you extend the camera lens by using bellows or extension tubes. In doing that, you must allow for an effective increase in the normal *f*/number or your picture will be underexposed.

You make such an exposure compensation whenever the subject distance is less than eight times the focal length of your lens.

This program provides a convenient means of determining the effective *f*/number. For example, if the focal length of your camera is 50mm and the lens-to-film distance (focal length plus extension from infinity position) is 100mm, and the normal *f*/stop would be 22, the corrected stop would be *f/11*.

Or, if you are using a 25mm lens, with 50mm lens-to-film distance, a normal *f*/stop of 8 should be corrected to *f/4*. Be sure to keep both focal length and distance in either mm or inches. Don't mix apples and oranges.

Program Listing

```
10 CALL CLEAR
20 PRINT "PHOTOGRAPHY: CLOSE UPS"
30 PRINT "**********************"
40 PRINT
50 INPUT "WHAT IS NORMAL F/number ":F
60 INPUT "LENS-TO-FILM DISTANCE IN MM ":D
70 IF D=0 THEN 60
80 INPUT "LENS FOCAL LENGTH IN MM ":L
100 N=F*L/D
200 PRINT
210 PRINT "EFFECTIVE F/number IS F/";N
220 FOR X=1 TO 5
230 PRINT
240 NEXT X
250 INPUT "TO DO MORE, PRESS ENTER":KY$
260 GOTO 10
```

Sample Run

```
PHOTOGRAPHY: CLOSE UPS
**********************

WHAT IS NORMAL F/number   22
LENS-TO-FILM DISTANCE IN MM    100
LENS FOCAL LENGTH IN MM   50

EFFECTIVE F/number IS F/ 11




TO DO MORE, PRESS ENTER
PHOTOGRAPHY: CLOSE UPS
**********************

WHAT IS NORMAL F/number    8
LENS-TO-FILM DISTANCE IN MM    50
LENS FOCAL LENGTH IN MM   25

EFFECTIVE F/number IS F/ 4
```

Math Flasher

Here's the basic routine (no pun intended) for an educational flash-card program. This one is bare-bones, no frills. You can dress it up with more colorful right-n-wrong messages, opening and closing billboards, etc. You could even make it keep score and present a "batting average" at the end of its run.

Here's how it works:

Lines 10 - 90 determine which type of math you wish to do. Lines 50 - 80 move program action to the appropriate group of lines further along in the program.

Lines 200-320 handle addition. Lines 400-530, subtraction. Lines 600-720, multiplication. Lines 800-940, division.

For example, look at lines 200-320. Two separate random numbers are generated (lines 200 and 210). The random numbers are labeled P and Q. At line 230, the program uses P and Q and asks you to add them together. Line 230 waits for and accepts your answer.

At line 260, the program makes the right or wrong decision, using the powerful IF/THEN statement. Line 300 prints the correct answer.

Program execution for subtract (lines 400-530), multiply (lines 600-720), and divide (lines 800-940), are similar except for line 420 in subtraction and line 830 in division.

We make the assumption that it is not desirable to have negative numbers as results of subtraction. That is, we want only subtraction problems with results of zero, one, two, three, or higher. We want no problems which would result in answers below zero such as -1, -2, -3, and so forth. So, line 420 tests P and Q, before presenting the problem on the screen. If they will result in a negative-number answer, then the program returns to lines 400-410 for two new numbers.

In division, we want whole-number answers. That is, we want answers like 2 or 11 or 26. Not answers like 1.81 or 9.75 or 21.3343. So, line 830 tests P and Q to make sure their dividend will be a whole number. If not, the program goes back to line 800 and line 810 for two new numbers.

Program Listing

```
10 RANDOMIZE
15 CALL CLEAR
20 PRINT "DO YOU WANT TO","ADD",
   "SUBTRACT","MULTIPLY","DIVIDE"
30 PRINT
40 INPUT "WHICH?":B$
50 IF B$="ADD" THEN 200
60 IF B$="SUBTRACT" THEN 400
70 IF B$="MULTIPLY" THEN 600
80 IF B$="DIVIDE" THEN 800
90 GOTO 40
200 P=INT(10*RND)
210 Q=INT(10*RND)
220 PRINT
230 PRINT "ADD ";P;" PLUS ";Q
240 INPUT R
250 PRINT
260 IF R=P+Q THEN 290
270 PRINT "WRONG"
280 GOTO 300
290 PRINT "RIGHT"
300 PRINT P;" PLUS ";Q;" EQUALS ";P+Q
310 PRINT
320 GOTO 200
400 P=INT(10*RND)
410 Q=INT(10*RND)
420 IF P-Q<0 THEN 400
430 PRINT
440 PRINT "SUBTRACT ";Q;" FROM ";P
450 INPUT R
460 PRINT
470 IF R=P-Q THEN 500
480 PRINT "WRONG"
490 GOTO 510
500 PRINT "RIGHT"
510 PRINT P;" MINUS ";Q;" EQUALS ";P-Q
520 PRINT
530 GOTO 400
600 P=INT(10*RND)
610 Q=INT(10*RND)
```

```
620 PRINT
630 PRINT "MULTIPLY ";P;" TIMES ";Q
640 INPUT R
650 PRINT
660 IF R=P*Q THEN 690
670 PRINT "WRONG"
680 GOTO 700
690 PRINT "RIGHT"
700 PRINT P;" TIMES ";Q;" EQUALS ";P*Q
710 PRINT
720 GOTO 600
800 P=INT(100*RND)
810 Q=INT(10*RND)
820 IF Q=0 THEN 810
830 IF (P/Q)<>INT(P/Q)THEN 800
840 PRINT
850 PRINT "DIVIDE ";P;" BY ";Q
860 INPUT R
870 PRINT
880 IF R=P/Q THEN 910
890 PRINT "WRONG"
900 GOTO 920
910 PRINT "RIGHT"
920 PRINT P;" DIVIDED BY ";Q;" EQUALS ";P/Q
930 PRINT
940 GOTO 800
```

Exam Score Sorting

The final number scores of a large number of test results can be categorized and thereby cut down into a smaller quantity of numbers easily.

This program accepts exam scores and divides them into ranges we have labeled A, B, C, D and F. The program looks for test scores in a range of zero to 100. The predetermined grade ranges are F=0 to 59; D=60 to 69; C=70 to 79; B=80 to 89; and A=90 to 100.

You key in the letter X to break the entry cycle. Lines 120 to 280 sort the scores into letter grades A through F. Lines 300 to 410 sort highest and lowest scores. Lines 500 -610 find the mid-range and average scores.

Program Listing

```
10 CALL CLEAR
20 PRINT "ENTER A GROUP OF SCORES"
30 PRINT "RANGING FROM ZERO TO 100"
40 PRINT "ONE AT A TIME."
50 PRINT
60 PRINT "ENTER X AFTER LAST SCORE"
70 PRINT
80 INPUT "SCORE: ":G$
90 IF G$="X" THEN 600
100 G=VAL(G$)
110 N=N+1
120 IF G<60 THEN 140
130 GOTO 160
140 F=F+1
150 GOTO 300
160 IF G<70 THEN 180
170 GOTO 200
180 D=D+1
190 GOTO 300
200 IF G<80 THEN 220
210 GOTO 240
220 C=C+1
230 GOTO 300
240 IF G<90 THEN 260
250 GOTO 280
260 B=B+1
270 GOTO 300
280 A=A+1
300 IF N=1 THEN 320
310 GOTO 350
320 L=G
330 H=G
340 GOTO 500
350 IF G<L THEN 370
360 GOTO 390
370 L=G
380 GOTO 500
390 IF G>H THEN 410
400 GOTO 500
410 H=G
```

```
500 S=S+G
510 GOTO 80
600 P=S/N
610 M=L+((H-L)/2)
700 CALL CLEAR
710 PRINT "A TOTAL OF ";N;" SCORES"
720 PRINT "RANGING FROM ";L;" TO ";H
730 PRINT "MID-RANGE SCORE IS ";M
740 PRINT "AVERAGE SCORE IS ";P
750 PRINT
760 PRINT "TOTALS FOR EACH LETTER:"
770 PRINT "A: ";A
780 PRINT "B: ";B
790 PRINT "C: ";C
800 PRINT "D: ";D
810 PRINT "F: ";F
900 PRINT
910 PRINT
920 PRINT
930 INPUT "TO DO MORE, PRESS RETURN":KY$
940 A=0
950 B=0
960 C=0
970 D=0
980 F=0
990 N=0
1000 L=0
1010 H=0
1020 M=0
1030 P=0
1040 G=0
1050 S=0
1060 G$=""
1070 GOTO 10
```

Sample Run

```
ENTER A GROUP OF SCORES
RANGING FROM ZERO TO 100
ONE AT A TIME.

ENTER X AFTER LAST SCORE
```

```
SCORE: 87
SCORE: 56
SCORE: 98
SCORE: 76
SCORE: 62
SCORE: 91
SCORE: 55
SCORE: 84
SCORE: 70
SCORE: 69
SCORE: 73
SCORE: X
A TOTAL OF   11   SCORES
RANGING FROM   55   TO   98
MID-RANGE SCORE IS   76.5
AVERAGE SCORE IS   74.63636364

TOTALS FOR EACH LETTER:
A:   2
B:   2
C:   3
D:   2
F:   2
```

Astronomy
Lightyears/Distance Conversions

Starlight,
Starbright,
I wish I may,
I wish I might,
Know the distance
To your light.

For students of astronomy everywhere, here's how to plug your computer into your hobby: use the machine to discover distances across the Universe!

This program converts lightyears to kilometers or kilometers to lightyears or lightyears to miles or miles to lightyears. It's hard to visualize distances in lightyears.

Run this program and you'll be better able to grasp the vast expanse of the Cosmos with your mind.

Of course, all distances are approximate. We use 365.86 days per year and, thus, 9.4830912×10^{12} km/ly or $5.892792872 \times 10^{12}$ mi/ly.

Program Listing

```
10 CALL CLEAR
20 GOSUB 410
30 PRINT "LIGHTYRS/DISTANCE CONVERSION"
40 GOSUB 410
50 PRINT
60 PRINT "YOUR CHOICES ARE:"
70 PRINT "(1) LIGHTYRS TO KILOMETERS"
80 PRINT "(2) LIGHTYRS TO MILES"
90 PRINT "(3) KILOMETERS TO LIGHTYRS"
100 PRINT "(4) MILES TO LIGHTYRS"
110 GOSUB 410
120 PRINT "WHICH CONVERSION: 1,2,3,4?"
130 CALL KEY(0,C,X)
140 IF X=0 THEN 130
150 IF C<49 THEN 120
160 IF C>52 THEN 120
170 IF C>50 THEN 310
180 PRINT
190 INPUT "LIGHTYEARS: ":L
200 K=L*(9.4830912*(10^12))
210 M=L*(5.89279287*(10^12))
220 CALL CLEAR
230 PRINT "LIGHTYEARS: ";L
240 IF C=50 THEN 290
250 PRINT "KILOMETERS: ";K
260 PRINT
270 PRINT
280 GOTO 50
290 PRINT "MILES:        ";M
300 GOTO 50
310 CALL CLEAR
320 IF C=52 THEN 370
330 INPUT "KILOMETERS: ":K
340 L=K/(9.4830912*(10^12))
```

```
350 PRINT "LIGHTYEARS:";L
360 GOTO 50
370 INPUT "MILES:       ":M
380 L=M/(5.89279287*(10^12))
390 GOTO 350
400 END
410 FOR Z=1 TO 28
420 PRINT "+";
430 NEXT Z
440 RETURN
```

State Geographic Centers

This mind bender tests your knowledge of geographic locations of cities and towns in the United States. These are special places since, in each case, they are the town nearest to the geographic center of its state.

In other words, Columbus happens to be almost exactly in the center of Ohio. But which state has Challis at its center? Or Lewistown? Or Oklahoma City? (Well, some may be obvious!)

You not only learn a lot from running this program but you have a barrel of fun. Talk about trivia!

Program Listing

```
10 CALL CLEAR
20 DATA CLANTON,ALABAMA
30 DATA MT. McKINLEY,ALASKA
40 DATA PRESCOTT,ARIZONA
50 DATA LITTLE ROCK,ARKANSAS
60 DATA MADERA,CALIFORNIA
70 DATA PIKES PEAK,COLORADO
80 DATA EAST BERLIN,CONNECTICUT
90 DATA DOVER,DELAWARE
100 DATA BROOKSVILLE,FLORIDA
110 DATA MACON,GEORGIA
120 DATA MAUI ISLAND,HAWAII
130 DATA CHALLIS,IDAHO
140 DATA SPRINGFIELD,ILLINOIS
```

```
150 DATA INDIANAPOLIS,INDIANA
160 DATA AMES,IOWA
170 DATA GREAT BANK,KANSAS
180 DATA LEBANON,KENTUCKY
190 DATA MARKSVILLE,LOUISIANA
200 DATA DOVER/FOXCROFT,MAINE
210 DATA DAVIDSONVILLE,MARYLAND
220 DATA WORCESTER,MASSACHUSETTS
230 DATA CADILLAC,MICHIGAN
240 DATA BRAINERD,MINNESOTA
250 DATA CARTHAGE,MISSISSIPPI
260 DATA JEFFERSON CITY,MISSOURI
270 DATA LEWISTOWN,MONTANA
280 DATA BROKEN BOW,NEBRASKA
290 DATA AUSTIN,NEVADA
300 DATA ASHLAND,NEW HAMPSHIRE
310 DATA TRENTON,NEW JERSEY
320 DATA WILLARD,NEW MEXICO
330 DATA ONEIDA,NEW YORK
340 DATA SANFORD,NORTH CAROLINA
350 DATA McCLUSKY,NORTH DAKOTA
360 DATA COLUMBUS,OHIO
370 DATA OKLAHOMA CITY,OKLAHOMA
380 DATA PRINEVILLE,OREGON
390 DATA BELLEFONTE,PENNSYLVANIA
400 DATA CROMPTON,RHODE ISLAND
410 DATA COLUMBIA,SOUTH CAROLINA
420 DATA PIERRE,SOUTH DAKOTA
430 DATA MURFREESBORO,TENNESSEE
440 DATA BRADY,TEXAS
450 DATA MANTI,UTAH
460 DATA ROXBURY,VERMONT
470 DATA BUCKINGHAM,VIRGINIA
480 DATA WENATCHEE,WASHINGTON
490 DATA SUTTON,WEST VIRGINIA
500 DATA MARSHFIELD,WISCONSIN
510 DATA LANDER,WYOMING
520 PRINT "FOR HOW MANY STATES"
530 PRINT "CAN YOU NAME"
540 PRINT "THE GEOGRAPHICAL CENTER?"
550 RANDOMIZE
560 R=INT(100*RND)
```

```
570 IF R<1 THEN 560
580 IF INT(R/2)=(R/2)THEN 600
590 GOTO 610
600 R=R-1
610 FOR L=1 TO R
620 READ S$
630 NEXT L
640 PRINT
650 PRINT
660 PRINT "WHICH STATE HAS ITS"
670 PRINT "GEOGRAPHIC CENTER NEAR"
680 PRINT S$
690 READ C$
700 INPUT D$
710 PRINT
720 IF C$=D$ THEN 740
730 GOTO 760
740 PRINT "THAT IS CORRECT"
750 GOTO 770
760 PRINT "SORRY, WRONG"
770 PRINT "THE CENTER OF ";C$
780 PRINT "IS ";S$
790 RESTORE
800 PRINT
810 PRINT
820 PRINT
830 GOTO 560
```

Sample Run

```
WHICH STATE HAS ITS
GEOGRAPHIC CENTER NEAR
WILLARD

NEW MEXICO

THAT IS CORRECT
THE CENTER OF NEW MEXICO
IS WILLARD
```

```
WHICH STATE HAS ITS
GEOGRAPHIC CENTER NEAR
BUCKINGHAM

CALIFORNIA

SORRY, WRONG
THE CENTER OF VIRGINIA
IS BUCKINGHAM


WHICH STATE HAS ITS
GEOGRAPHIC CENTER NEAR
LEWISTOWN

MONTANA

THAT IS CORRECT
THE CENTER OF MONTANA
IS LEWISTOWN
```

Volumes

Cones. Cubes. Cylinders. Prisms. Pyramids. Spheres. Name your object. This program computes the volume and displays it in cubic units.

Put in inches, get cubic inches. Put in feet, get cubic feet. Yards, get cubic yards. No mixing units in any one calculation. Cylinder is right circular.

Program Listing

```
10 CALL CLEAR
20 INPUT "WHAT IS THE OBJECT?":X$
30 IF X$="CONE" THEN 100
40 IF X$="CUBE" THEN 200
50 IF X$="CYLINDER" THEN 300
60 IF X$="PRISM" THEN 400
```

```
70 IF X$="PYRAMID" THEN 100
80 IF X$="SPHERE" THEN 500
90 GOTO 20
100 INPUT "AREA = ":A
110 INPUT "HEIGHTH = ":H
120 V=(A*H)/3
130 GOTO 600
200 INPUT "LENGTH = ":L
210 INPUT "WIDTH = ":W
220 INPUT "HEIGHTH = ":H
230 V=L*W*H
240 GOTO 600
300 INPUT "RADIUS = ":R
310 INPUT "HEIGHTH = ":H
320 V=3.141592654*2*R*H
330 GOTO 600
400 INPUT "AREA = ":A
410 INPUT "HEIGHTH = ":H
420 V=A*H
430 GOTO 600
500 INPUT "RADIUS = ":R
510 V=(3.141592654*4*(R^3))/3
600 PRINT
610 PRINT "VOLUME = ";V
620 PRINT
630 PRINT
640 GOTO 20
```

Sample Run

```
WHAT IS THE OBJECT? PRISM
AREA =   71
HEIGHTH =   18

VOLUME =   1278


WHAT IS THE OBJECT? CUBE
LENGTH =   13
WIDTH =   8
HEIGHTH =   24

VOLUME =   2496
```

```
WHAT IS THE OBJECT? CONE
AREA =  55
HEIGHT =  66

VOLUME =  1210


WHAT IS THE OBJECT? CYLINDER
RADIUS =  88
HEIGHT =  33

VOLUME =  18246.37013


WHAT IS THE OBJECT? SPHERE
RADIUS =  1234

VOLUME =  7871075686.


WHAT IS THE OBJECT? PYRAMID
AREA =  321
HEIGHT =  22

VOLUME =  2354
```

Event Timer

Place your computer in a corner and let it time your next chess match. Three-minute egg. Final exam.

The computer asks how many minutes you want for the event you are timing, and then it sounds a bell when the time has passed.

You can calibrate the clock by changing the value of SP in line 10. A larger number will slow down the clock. A smaller value for SP will speed up the clock. As you can see we have started with an SP value of 25.

If you want to time an event of less than one minute, use a decimal. For instance, when you want to time a 30-second event, respond to the computer's inquiry with .5 or for 45 seconds key in .75. Use .17 for 10 seconds; .25 for 15 seconds.

Program Listing

```
10 SP=25
20 CALL CLEAR
30 PRINT "EVENT TIMER"
40 PRINT "***********"
50 PRINT "HOW MANY MINUTES"
60 INPUT "TO THE END OF THE EVENT?":LT
70 PRINT
80 SP=SP/10
90 INPUT "TO START TIMING, PRESS ENTER":ST$
100 CALL CLEAR
110 C=C+1
120 IF C>(SP*LT*60)THEN 170
130 MN=INT(C/SP/60)
140 SC=INT((C/SP)-(60*MN))
150 PRINT MN;" MINUTES ";SC;" SECONDS"
160 GOTO 110
170 CALL CLEAR
180 CALL SOUND(100,150,0)
190 PRINT "TIME IS UP"
200 PRINT LT;" MINUTES HAVE PASSED"
210 PRINT
220 PRINT
230 PRINT
240 INPUT "TO TIME AGAIN, PRESS ENTER":KY$
250 C=0
260 GOTO 10
```

U.S. Presidents

Fourteenth. Let's see, that was Franklin Pierce. *Correct. The fourteenth president was Franklin Pierce.* Let's try another. *Thirty-fourth.* John F. Kennedy. *Wrong. The thirty-fourth president was Dwight D. Eisenhower.*

How many of the 40 U.S. presidents can you name? Bet not as many as you would like!

This program tests not only your knowledge of the

name of each president and his number in rank, but also the spelling of his name.

The more you take this test, the more you learn.

Program Listing

```
10 CALL CLEAR
20 RANDOMIZE
30 DATA FIRST,GEORGE WASHINGTON
40 DATA SECOND,JOHN ADAMS
50 DATA THIRD,THOMAS JEFFERSON
60 DATA FOURTH,JAMES MADISON
70 DATA FIFTH,JAMES MONROE
80 DATA SIXTH,JOHN QUINCY ADAMS
90 DATA SEVENTH,ANDREW JACKSON
100 DATA EIGHTH,MARTIN VAN BUREN
110 DATA NINTH,WILLIAM H. HARRISON
120 DATA TENTH,JOHN TYLER
130 DATA ELEVENTH,JAMES K. POLK
140 DATA TWELFTH,ZACHARY TAYLOR
150 DATA THIRTEENTH,MILLARD FILLMORE
160 DATA FOURTEENTH,FRANKLIN PIERCE
170 DATA FIFTEENTH,JAMES BUCHANAN
180 DATA SIXTEENTH,ABRAHAM LINCOLN
190 DATA SEVENTEENTH,ANDREW JOHNSON
200 DATA EIGHTEENTH,ULYSSES S. GRANT
210 DATA NINTEENTH,RUTHERFORD B. HAYES
220 DATA TWENTIETH,JAMES A. GARFIELD
230 DATA TWENTY-FIRST,CHESTER A. ARTHUR
240 DATA TWENTY-SECOND,GROVER CLEVELAND
250 DATA TWENTY-THIRD,BENJAMIN HARRISON
260 DATA TWENTY-FOURTH,GROVER CLEVELAND
270 DATA TWENTY-FIFTH,WILLIAM MCKINLEY
280 DATA TWENTY-SIXTH,THEODORE ROOSEVELT
290 DATA TWENTY-SEVENTH,WILLIAM H. TAFT
300 DATA TWENTY-EIGHTH,WOODROW WILSON
310 DATA TWENTY-NINTH,WARREN G. HARDING
320 DATA THIRTIETH,CALVIN COOLIDGE
330 DATA THIRTY-FIRST,HERBERT HOOVER
340 DATA THIRTY-SECOND,FRANKLIN D. ROOSEVELT
350 DATA THIRTY-THIRD,HARRY S TRUMAN
360 DATA THIRTY-FOURTH,DWIGHT D. EISENHOWER
```

```
370 DATA THIRTY-FIFTH,JOHN F. KENNEDY
380 DATA THIRTY-SIXTH,LYNDON B. JOHNSON
390 DATA THIRTY-SEVENTH,RICHARD M. NIXON
400 DATA THIRTY-EIGHTH,GERALD R. FORD
410 DATA THIRTY-NINTH,JIMMY CARTER
420 DATA FOURTIETH,RONALD REAGAN
430 PRINT "*******************"
440 PRINT "* U.S. PRESIDENTS *"
450 PRINT "*******************"
460 PRINT
470 PRINT "HOW MANY CAN YOU NAME?"
480 FOR Q=1 TO 11
490 PRINT
500 NEXT Q
510 PRINT "PRESS ANY KEY TO START"
520 CALL KEY(0,Z,X)
530 IF X=0 THEN 520
540 CALL CLEAR
550 R=INT(81*RND)
560 IF R<1 THEN 550
570 IF INT(R/2)=(R/2)THEN 590
580 GOTO 600
590 R=R-1
600 FOR L=1 TO R
610 READ S$
620 NEXT L
630 PRINT "WHO WAS THE"
640 PRINT S$
650 PRINT "PRESIDENT OF THE"
660 READ C$
670 INPUT "UNITED STATES? ":D$
680 PRINT
690 PRINT
700 IF D$=C$ THEN 730
710 PRINT "WRONG"
720 GOTO 740
730 PRINT "CORRECT"
740 PRINT "THE ";S$;" PRESIDENT"
750 PRINT "WAS ";C$
760 RESTORE
770 PRINT
780 PRINT
```

```
790 PRINT "FOR MORE, PRESS M"
800 PRINT "TO QUIT,  PRESS Q"
810 CALL KEY(O,Z,X)
820 IF X=O THEN 810
830 IF Z=77 THEN 540
840 IF Z=81 THEN 860
850 GOTO 780
860 CALL CLEAR
870 PRINT "END OF TEST"
880 PRINT "***********"
890 PRINT "THANK YOU"
900 PRINT
910 PRINT
```

Sample Run

```
********************
* U.S. PRESIDENTS *
********************
HOW MANY CAN YOU NAME?
PRESS ANY KEY TO START

WHO WAS THE
SEVENTH
PRESIDENT OF THE
UNITED STATES?
ANDREW JACKSON
CORRECT
THE SEVENTH PRESIDENT
WAS ANDREW JACKSON

FOR MORE, PRESS M
TO QUIT,  PRESS Q

WHO WAS THE
THIRTY-THIRD
PRESIDENT OF THE
UNITED STATES?
HARRY S TRUMAN
CORRECT
THE THIRTY-THIRD PRESIDENT
WAS HARRY S TRUMAN

FOR MORE, PRESS M
TO QUIT,  PRESS Q
```

Class Roll Sorter

Here's a simple sorting routine which you can use to keep your class roll in order. Suppose it's the first day of classes and you have been handed an unorganized list of student names. Merely key those names into the computer and it will use this "bubble sort" program to put the list in alphabetical order. As set up, it accepts up to 20 names.

The size of the list is controlled by the DIM instruction in line 20. You can change it. The more names to sort, the longer it takes.

Of course, you can change names to other categories such as items, products, units, etc.

Program Listing

```
10 CALL CLEAR
20 DIM M$(20)
30 FOR L=1 TO 20
40 INPUT "NAME: ":M$(L)
50 IF M$(L)="" THEN 70
60 NEXT L
70 CALL CLEAR
80 PRINT "SORTING NOW"
90 T=0
100 FOR L=1 TO 19
110 IF M$(L)<=M$(L+1)THEN 160
120 E$=M$(L)
130 M$(L)=M$(L+1)
140 M$(L+1)=E$
150 T=1
160 NEXT L
170 IF T=1 THEN 90
180 CALL CLEAR
190 CALL SOUND(2,1000,1)
200 FOR L=1 TO 20
210 IF M$(L)<>"" THEN 230
220 GOTO 240
230 PRINT M$(L)
240 NEXT L
```

Program Listing

```
1 REM *****THIS VERSION OF THE
2 REM *****PROGRAM PRINTS THE
3 REM *****SORTED LIST ON THE
4 REM *****99/4 IMPACT PRINTER
5 REM *****
6 REM *****ONLY CHANGES ARE
7 REM *****TO LINE 230
8 REM *****AND ADDING LINE 15
9 REM *****
10 CALL CLEAR
15 OPEN #1:"RS232"
20 DIM M$(20)
30 FOR L=1 TO 20
40  INPUT "NAME: ":M$(L)
50  IF M$(L)="" THEN 70
60 NEXT L
70 CALL CLEAR
80 PRINT "SORTING NOW"
90 T=0
100 FOR L=1 TO 19
110 IF M$(L)<=M$(L+1)THEN 160
120 E$=M$(L)
130 M$(L)=M$(L+1)
140 M$(L+1)=E$
150 T=1
160 NEXT L
170 IF T=1 THEN 90
180 CALL CLEAR
190 CALL SOUND(2,1000,1)
200 FOR L=1 TO 20
210 IF M$(L)<>"" THEN 230
220 GOTO 240
230 PRINT #1:M$(L)
240 NEXT L
```

Sample Run

```
NAME: FRED
NAME: ANDY
NAME: ZITA
```

```
NAME: BOB
NAME: HELEN
NAME: RONDA
NAME: MIKE
NAME: ALLAN
NAME: ALLEN
NAME: CHARLES
NAME: PAULA
NAME: TOM
NAME: PAUL
NAME:
SORTING NOW
ALLAN
ALLEN
ANDY
BOB
CHARLES
FRED
HELEN
MIKE
PAUL
PAULA
RONDA
TOM
ZITA

NAME: SMITH BOB
NAME: SMITH HELEN
NAME: SMITH CLYDE
NAME: SMITH MOLLY
NAME: SMITH GREG
NAME: SMITH JACK
NAME: SMITH AUDRY
NAME:
SORTING NOW
SMITH AUDRY
SMITH BOB
SMITH CLYDE
SMITH GREG
SMITH HELEN
SMITH JACK
SMITH MOLLY
```

```
 !"#$%&'()*+,-./0123456789:;<=>?@ABCDEI
!"#$%&'()*+,-./0123456789:;<=>?@ABCDEF(
"#$%&'()*+,-./0123456789:;<=>?@ABCDEFGI
#$%&'()*+,-./0123456789:;<=>?@ABCDEFGH
$%&'()*+,-./0123456789:;<=>?@ABCDEFGHI.
%&'()*+,-./0123456789:;<=>?@ABCDEFGHIJI
&'()*+,-./0123456789:;<=>?@ABCDEFGHIJKI
'()*+,-./0123456789:;<=>?@ABCDEFGHIJKLI
()*+,-./0123456789:;<=>?@ABCDEFGHIJKLMI
)*+,-./0123456789:;<=>?@ABCDEFGHIJKLMN(
*+,-./0123456789:;<=>?@ABCDEFGHIJKLMNOI
+,-./0123456789:;<=>?@ABCDEFGHIJKLMNOP(
,-./0123456789:;<=>?@ABCDEFGHIJKLMNOPQI
-./0123456789:;<=>?@ABCDEFGHIJKLMNOPQR!
./0123456789:;<=>?@ABCDEFGHIJKLMNOPQRS'
/0123456789:;<=>?@ABCDEFGHIJKLMNOPQRSTI
0123456789:;<=>?@ABCDEFGHIJKLMNOPQRSTU'
123456789:;<=>?@ABCDEFGHIJKLMNOPQRSTUVI
23456789:;<=>?@ABCDEFGHIJKLMNOPQRSTUVW
3456789:;<=>?@ABCDEFGHIJKLMNOPQRSTUVWX'
456789:;<=>?@ABCDEFGHIJKLMNOPQRSTUVWXY
56789:;<=>?@ABCDEFGHIJKLMNOPQRSTUVWXYZ
6789:;<=>?@ABCDEFGHIJKLMNOPQRSTUVWXYZ[
789:;<=>?@ABCDEFGHIJKLMNOPQRSTUVWXYZ[\
89:;<=>?@ABCDEFGHIJKLMNOPQRSTUVWXYZ[\]·
9:;<=>?@ABCDEFGHIJKLMNOPQRSTUVWXYZ[\]^.
:;<=>?@ABCDEFGHIJKLMNOPQRSTUVWXYZ[\]^_
;<=>?@ABCDEFGHIJKLMNOPQRSTUVWXYZ[\]^_`.
<=>?@ABCDEFGHIJKLMNOPQRSTUVWXYZ[\]^_`al
=>?@ABCDEFGHIJKLMNOPQRSTUVWXYZ[\]^_`ab
>?@ABCDEFGHIJKLMNOPQRSTUVWXYZ[\]^_`abc
?@ABCDEFGHIJKLMNOPQRSTUVWXYZ[\]^_`abcd
@ABCDEFGHIJKLMNOPQRSTUVWXYZ[\]^_`abcde
ABCDEFGHIJKLMNOPQRSTUVWXYZ[\]^_`abcdef
BCDEFGHIJKLMNOPQRSTUVWXYZ[\]^_`abcdefg
CDEFGHIJKLMNOPQRSTUVWXYZ[\]^_`abcdefgh
DEFGHIJKLMNOPQRSTUVWXYZ[\]^_`abcdefghi
EFGHIJKLMNOPQRSTUVWXYZ[\]^_`abcdefghij
FGHIJKLMNOPQRSTUVWXYZ[\]^_`abcdefghijk
GHIJKLMNOPQRSTUVWXYZ[\]^_`abcdefghijkl
HIJKLMNOPQRSTUVWXYZ[\]^_`abcdefghijklm
IJKLMNOPQRSTUVWXYZ[\]^_`abcdefghijklmn
```

Programs
for the business person

Profit Estimator

How much cash flow will I generate if I sell 100 thingamabobs? A question faced everyday in the business office. Whether you sell large lots at wholesale, small quantities across the retail counter, or individual items via mail order, this program will give you a quick estimate of expected cash flow and potential profits. It allows fast comparisons when quick decisions are needed.

The computer asks you questions about the quantity of items involved, prices, quantity sold, discounts, etc. Then it calculates unit price, unit profit, gross profit, return percentages, sales needed to break even, and more, depending upon which part of the program you are using.

The program is divided into four main blocks:

—an opening billboard from line 10 through line 180;
—wholesale computations, lines 1000 to 1320;
—mail order computations, lines 2000 to 2360;
—ad response computations, lines 3000 to 3590.

Remember that the program only *estimates*, it is not exact. The wholesale, direct-mail, or ad-response manufacturing cost asked by the computer is *total*, not per unit.

This program is a useful tool for small business, whether a local furniture store, supermarket, wholesaler, or regional mail-order house.

Program Listing

```
10 CALL CLEAR
20 PRINT "PROFIT ESTIMATOR"
30 PRINT
40 PRINT "WHICH TYPE OF SALE:"
50 PRINT "(W)  WHOLESALE"
60 PRINT "(D)  DIRECT MAIL"
70 PRINT "(M)  MEDIA AD RESPONSE"
80 PRINT
90 PRINT "W, D OR M ? "
100 CALL KEY(0,Z,X)
110 IF X=0 THEN 100
120 IF Z=87 THEN 1000
```

```
130 IF Z=68 THEN 2000
140 IF Z=77 THEN 3000
150 PRINT "OKAY, YOU SELECTED ";CHR$(Z)
160 PRINT "HOWEVER, ";CHR$(Z);" IS"
170 PRINT "NOT A CHOICE. TRY AGAIN"
180 GOTO 90
1000 CALL CLEAR
1010 PRINT "WHOLESALE PROFIT ESTIMATOR"
1020 PRINT "****************************"
1030 PRINT "PLEASE ANSWER SOME QUESTIONS"
1040 PRINT "WHAT IS"
1050 INPUT "MANUFACTURING COST $":C
1060 INPUT "QUANTITY MANUFACTURED ":P
1070 INPUT "LIST PRICE OF ITEM $":L
1080 INPUT "TOTAL QUANTITY SOLD ":S
1090 IF S<>0 THEN 1110
1100 GOTO 10
1110 INPUT "WHOLESALE DISCOUNT % ":D
1120 UC=C/P
1130 UP=(L*((100-D)/100))-UC
1140 W=L*S*((100-D)/100)
1150 G=W-(S*UC)
1160 CALL CLEAR
1170 PRINT "---------------------"
1180 PRINT "UNIT COST IS $";UC
1190 PRINT "UNIT PROFIT IS $";UP
1200 PRINT "WHOLESALE GROSS $";W
1210 PRINT "WHOLESALE PROFIT $";G
1220 PRINT "---------------------"
1320 GOTO 4000
2000 CALL CLEAR
2010 PRINT "DIRECT MAIL"
2020 PRINT "PROFIT ESTIMATOR"
2030 PRINT "*****************"
2040 PRINT "PLEASE ANSWER SOME QUESTIONS"
2050 PRINT "WHAT IS THE"
2060 INPUT "MANUFACTURING COST $":C
2065 INPUT "QUANTITY MANUFACTURED ":P
2070 INPUT "LIST PRICE OF ITEM $":L
2080 INPUT "TOTAL QUANITY SOLD ":S
2090 INPUT "NUMBER OF FLYERS MAILED ":K
2100 INPUT "FLYER PRINTING COST $":R
```

```
2110 INPUT "POSTAGE COST $":M
2120 UC=C/P
2130 J=100*S/K
2140 T=L*S-(R+M+UC*S)
2150 U=L*S
2160 CALL CLEAR
2170 PRINT "--------------------"
2180 PRINT "DIRECT MAIL"
2190 PRINT "RETURN IS ";J;" PERCENT"
2200 PRINT "DIRECT MAIL GROSS $";U
2210 PRINT "DIRECT MAIL PROFIT $";T
2220 PRINT "--------------------"
2360 GOTO 4000
3000 CALL CLEAR
3010 PRINT "RESPONSE TO ADVERTISEMENT"
3020 PRINT "PROFIT ESTIMATOR"
3030 PRINT "*************************"
3040 PRINT "PLEASE ANSWER SOME QUESTIONS"
3050 PRINT "WHAT IS THE"
3060 INPUT "MANUFACTURING COST $":C
3070 INPUT "QUANTITY MANUFACTURED ":P
3080 INPUT "LIST PRICE OF ITEM $":L
3090 INPUT "AD COST PER INSERTION $":A
3100 INPUT "NUMBER OF INSERTIONS ":I
3110 PRINT
3120 PRINT
3130 PRINT "WHICH DO YOU WANT TO KNOW?"
3140 PRINT
3150 PRINT "(Q) SALES QUANTITY"
3160 PRINT "    NEEDED TO BREAK EVEN"
3170 PRINT "(P) PROFIT FROM SELLING"
3180 PRINT "    A SPECIFIC QUANTITY"
3190 PRINT
3200 PRINT "P OR Q ?"
3210 CALL KEY(0,Z,X)
3220 IF X=0 THEN 3210
3230 IF Z=80 THEN 3400
3240 IF Z=81 THEN 3270
3250 PRINT "PLEASE PRESS P OR Q"
3260 GOTO 3210
3270 B=INT((C+A*I)/L)+1
3280 CALL CLEAR
```

```
3290 PRINT "———————————————————"
3300 PRINT "SELL ";B;" TO BREAK EVEN"
3310 PRINT "INCLUDING COVERING"
3320 PRINT "$";C;" MANUFACTURING COST"
3330 PRINT "AND $";A*I;" AD CAMPAIGN"
3340 PRINT "———————————————————"
3350 GOTO 4000
3400 PRINT
3410 INPUT "QUANTITY SOLD ":S
3420 N=S*L
3430 UC=C/P
3440 E=S*L-S*UC-A*I
3450 CALL CLEAR
3460 PRINT "———————————————————"
3470 PRINT "ORDERS GROSS IS $";N
3480 PRINT "DIRECT MAIL PROFIT IS $";E
3590 PRINT "———————————————————"
4000 PRINT
4010 PRINT
4020 PRINT "TO DO MORE, PRESS M"
4030 PRINT "TO QUIT, PRESS Q"
4040 CALL KEY(0,Z,X)
4050 IF X=0 THEN 4040
4060 IF Z=77 THEN 10
4070 IF Z=81 THEN 4090
4080 GOTO 4010
4090 CALL CLEAR
4100 PRINT "OKAY, BYE BYE"
4110 PRINT
4120 PRINT
4130 PRINT
4140 END
```

Daily Codes

Businesses everywhere are concerned about security. Banks, credit card managers, warehousemen, shipping clerks, office managers, all need private daily codes for internal use to prevent unauthorized admission to storage areas, financial records, private files.

Now you can use your own computer to generate a set of secret codes, one for each day of the week. This program generates a series of pseudorandom numbers and displays a table of those numbers alongside names of the days of the week.

The subroutine in lines 300 to 330 generates four-digit random numbers.

Program Listing

```
10 CALL CLEAR
20 GOSUB 300
30 PRINT "SUNDAY:      ";C
40 GOSUB 300
50 PRINT "MONDAY:      ";C
60 GOSUB 300
70 PRINT "TUESDAY:     ";C
80 GOSUB 300
90 PRINT "WEDNESDAY: ";C
100 GOSUB 300
110 PRINT "THURSDAY:    ";C
120 GOSUB 300
130 PRINT "FRIDAY:      ";C
140 GOSUB 300
150 PRINT "SATURDAY:    ";C
200 PRINT
205 PRINT
210 PRINT
215 PRINT
220 PRINT
225 PRINT
230 PRINT "FOR A DIFFERENT SET"
240 PRINT "OF NUMBERS,"
250 PRINT "PRESS ANY KEY"
260 CALL KEY(0,Z,X)
270 IF X=0 THEN 260
280 GOTO 10
300 RANDOMIZE
310 C=INT(10000*RND)
320 IF C<1000 THEN 310
330 RETURN
```

Program Listing

```
1 REM *****THIS VERSION OF THE
2 REM *****DAILY CODES PROGRAM
3 REM *****PROVIDES A HARDCOPY
4 REM *****PRINTOUT OF THE CHART
5 REM ***************************
10 OPEN #1:"RS232"
15 CALL CLEAR
20 GOSUB 300
30 PRINT #1:"SUNDAY:     ";C
40 GOSUB 300
50 PRINT #1:"MONDAY:     ";C
60 GOSUB 300
70 PRINT #1:"TUESDAY:    ";C
80 GOSUB 300
90 PRINT #1:"WEDNESDAY: ";C
100 GOSUB 300
110 PRINT #1:"THURSDAY:   ";C
120 GOSUB 300
130 PRINT #1:"FRIDAY:     ";C
140 GOSUB 300
150 PRINT #1:"SATURDAY:   ";C
200 PRINT #1
230 PRINT #1:"FOR A DIFFERENT SET"
240 PRINT #1:"OF NUMBERS,"
250 PRINT #1:"PRESS ANY KEY"
260 CALL KEY(0,Z,X)
270 IF X=0 THEN 260
280 PRINT #1
285 PRINT #1
290 GOTO 15
300 RANDOMIZE
310 C=INT(10000*RND)
320 IF C<1000 THEN 310
330 RETURN
```

Sample Run

```
SUNDAY:     6321
MONDAY:     9105
TUESDAY:    2612
WEDNESDAY:  2482
```

```
THURSDAY:     2415
FRIDAY:       7389
SATURDAY:     7989

FOR A DIFFERENT SET
OF NUMBERS,
PRESS ANY KEY


SUNDAY:       7182
MONDAY:       3586
TUESDAY:      8637
WEDNESDAY:    9057
THURSDAY:     8205
FRIDAY:       2500
SATURDAY:     9779

FOR A DIFFERENT SET
OF NUMBERS,
PRESS ANY KEY
```

Invoice Computer

The computer will ask you for a discount percentage to be applied to the invoice; the retail price of goods being invoiced; and the quantity of those goods.

You enter actual percentage. The computer changes that to the appropriate decimal vaue.

Then it will ask if you have other items to be shown on the same invoice. If so, it again will get price and quantity sold info from you. It will assume the same discount applies.

When you tell the computer there are no more items for the same invoice, it will compute and display the total.

Program Listing

```
10 GOSUB 470
20 PRINT "INFO NEEDED"
30 PRINT "FOR COMPUTING INVOICES:"
40 PRINT
50 INPUT "DISCOUNT PERCENTAGE % ":DP
```

```
60 DD=1-0.01*DP
70 PRINT
80 INPUT "NAME OF ITEM SOLD: ":IT$
90 INPUT "RETAIL PRICE $":P
100 INPUT "QUANTITY SOLD: ":Q
110 C=P*DD
120 I=C*Q
130 T=T+I
140 PRINT
150 PRINT
160 PRINT "WHOLESALE COST"
170 PRINT "OF";Q;;IT$;"'S: $";I
180 PRINT
190 PRINT
200 PRINT "MORE ON SAME INVOICE?"
210 PRINT "IF MORE, PRESS M"
220 PRINT "IF NO MORE, PRESS Q"
230 CALL KEY(0,Z,X)
240 IF X=0 THEN 230
250 IF Z=77 THEN 70
260 IF Z=81 THEN 280
270 GOTO 210
280 PRINT
290 PRINT "INVOICE GRAND TOTAL $";T
300 PRINT
310 PRINT
320 PRINT "TO DO OTHER INVOICES,"
330 PRINT "AT OTHER DISCOUNTS,"
340 PRINT "PRESS M."
350 PRINT "TO QUIT, PRESS Q"
360 CALL KEY(0,Z,X)
370 IF X=0 THEN 360
380 IF Z=77 THEN 410
390 IF Z=81 THEN 430
400 GOTO 320
410 T=0
420 GOTO 10
430 CALL CLEAR
440 PRINT "OKAY, BYE BYE"
450 END
460 END
470 CALL CLEAR
```

```
480 PRINT "********************"
490 PRINT "* INVOICE COMPUTER *"
500 PRINT "********************"
510 PRINT
520 RETURN
```

Hourly Wages

This handy program computes total hours worked at regular pay and number of hours worked at time-and-a-half overtime. It then finds gross pay and rounds off to the nearest cent. The program knows that overtime starts after 40 hours.

The result is a nice chart on the display, after the computer asks only three questions.

You can change the number of regular-work hours per week by changing the number 40 in lines 200 and 210. Change the overtime multiplier of 1.5 by changing the number 1.5 in line 300.

This program makes payroll booking quick and simple.

Program Listing

```
10 CALL CLEAR
20 PRINT "****************"
30 PRINT "* HOURLY WAGES *"
40 PRINT "****************"
50 PRINT
60 INPUT "EMPLOYEE'S NAME: ":N$
70 INPUT "HOURLY PAY RATE $":P
80 INPUT "TOTAL HOURS WORKED: ":H
200 IF H<=40 THEN 220
210 IF H>40 THEN 250
220 RH=H
230 OH=0
240 GOTO 300
250 OH=H-40
260 RH=40
300 OP=1.5*P
310 PA=RH*P
320 PB=OH*OP
```

```
330 PY=PA+PB
340 PY=INT(100*PY+0.5)/100
400 CALL CLEAR
410 PRINT "EMPLOYEE: ";N$
420 PRINT
430 PRINT "TOTAL HOURS: ";H
440 PRINT
450 PRINT "REGULAR HOURS: ";RH
460 PRINT "REGULAR RATE: $";P
470 PRINT "TOTAL REGULAR PAY: $";PA
480 PRINT
490 PRINT "OVERTIME HOURS: ";OH
500 PRINT "OVERTIME RATE $";OP
510 PRINT "TOTAL OVERTIME: $";PB
520 PRINT
530 PRINT "GROSS PAY: $";PY
600 FOR L=1 TO 4
610 PRINT
620 NEXT L
630 PRINT "TO COMPUTE WAGES"
640 PRINT "FOR A DIFFERENT EMPLOYEE"
650 PRINT "PRESS ANY KEY"
660 CALL KEY(0,Z,X)
670 IF X=0 THEN 660
680 GOTO 10
```

Sample Run

```
*****************
* HOURLY WAGES *
*****************

EMPLOYEE'S NAME: JONES
HOURLY PAY RATE $ 5
TOTAL HOURS WORKED:   50
EMPLOYEE: JONES
TOTAL HOURS:   50
REGULAR HOURS:   40
REGULAR RATE: $ 5
TOTAL REGULAR PAY: $ 200
OVERTIME HOURS:   10
OVERTIME RATE $ 7.5
```

```
TOTAL OVERTIME: $ 75
GROSS PAY: $ 275

TO COMPUTE WAGES
FOR A DIFFERENT EMPLOYEE
PRESS ANY KEY
```

Ad Campaign Profit

The ad salesman is standing in your office pressing for your answer. Do you want to advertise or not? Advertising costs plenty of money today. How can you make a quick decision about whether or not sales from advertising would be worth the cost?

In this program, the computer asks you for information about the list price of the item you would sell through advertising. It asks for the manufacturing cost of that item; the cost of the advertising campaign; and the number of units sold.

It computes your gross sales and deducts the cost of manufacturing and advertising to show an estimate of profits to be expected. If you key in a zero in response to the number-sold question, the machine will inquire as to the amount of profit you would like to make and then tell you how many units you would have to sell to make such a profit.

If you would like to make your own changes to this program listing, you'll want to know that memory location B holds the list price of the item you are selling; C is the unit manufacturing cost of the item; D is the total advertising cost; A is the number of units sold of the item; E is the profit on the sales of the item; and F is the profit you say you want to make.

Suppose you have an item you sell for $9.95 and it costs you $1.25 to produce it. An ad campaign costing $330 results in sales of 50 units. Your profit from the campaign would be $105. If you only wanted to know how many units you would have to sell to break even, enter zero in response to the number-sold question and $1 to the profit-wanted question. You'll discover you need to sell just over 38 units to break even.

Program Listing

```
10 CALL CLEAR
20 INPUT "LIST: $":B
30 INPUT "MANUFACTURING COST: $":C
40 INPUT "ADVERTISING COST: $":D
50 INPUT "QUANTITY SOLD: ":A
60 IF A=0 THEN 200
70 E=A*B-A*C-D
80 PRINT
90 PRINT
100 PRINT "PROFIT: $";E
110 PRINT
120 PRINT
130 GOTO 50
200 INPUT "PROFIT WANTED: $":F
210 A=(F+D)/(B-C)
220 PRINT
230 PRINT
240 PRINT "SELL:   ";A
250 PRINT "PROFIT: $";F
260 PRINT
270 PRINT
280 GOTO 50
```

Sample Run

```
LIST: $ 9.95
MANUFACTURING COST: $ 1.25
ADVERTISING COST: $ 330
QUANTITY SOLD:  50

PROFIT: $ 105

QUANTITY SOLD:  0
PROFIT WANTED: $ 1

SELL:    38.04597701
PROFIT: $ 1

QUANTITY SOLD:  1000

PROFIT: $ 8370
```

Media Money Massage

If you have used the *Ad Campaign Profit* program earlier in this book, you know how many bucks you can expect to make from advertising. But, suppose two salesmen are standing in your office. One from your local newspaper and the other from a local television station. Both want your advertising dollar and you can't decide which is the best buy.

This program compares the cost of advertising in two media and reports which is most favorable. First it computes cost-per-thousand. Then it highlights the least-expensive medium.

And, it compares any media—newspaper, radio, television, magazines, shoppers, etc.

Imagine your friendly salesmen are from the Daily Post and the Evening News. The ad in the Post costs $250. In the News it is $300. The Post's circulation is 27,500 readers. The News has 32,500 readers. Which is the better buy? The Post is about 14¢ cheaper per thousand readers.

Program Listing

```
10 CALL CLEAR
20 INPUT "FIRST MEDIUM: ":N$
30 INPUT "ADVERTISING COST: $":A
40 INPUT "CIRCULATION: ":C
50 M=1000*(A/C)
60 PRINT
70 INPUT "SECOND MEDIUM: ":P$
80 INPUT "ADVERTISING COST: $":Q
90 INPUT "CIRCULATION: ":R
100 S=1000*(Q/R)
110 CALL CLEAR
120 IF S>M THEN 140
130 IF M>S THEN 190
140 PRINT N$
150 PRINT "HAS A LOWER"
160 PRINT "COST PER THOUSAND"
170 PRINT "AT $";M
```

```
180 GOTO 230
190 PRINT P$
200 PRINT "HAS A LOWER"
210 PRINT "COST PER THOUSAND"
220 PRINT "AT $";S
230 PRINT
240 PRINT N$
250 PRINT "CPM: $";M
260 PRINT "ADVERTISING: $";A
270 PRINT "CIRCULATION: ";C
280 PRINT
290 PRINT P$
300 PRINT "CPM: $";S
310 PRINT "ADVERTISING: $";Q
320 PRINT "CIRCULATION: ";R
330 PRINT
340 PRINT
350 PRINT "TO DO MORE, PRESS ANY KEY"
360 CALL KEY(0,Z,X)
370 IF X=0 THEN 360
380 GOTO 10
```

Sample Run

```
FIRST MEDIUM: POST
ADVERTISING COST: $ 250
CIRCULATION:   27500

SECOND MEDIUM: NEWS
ADVERTISING COST: $ 300
CIRCULATION:   32500
POST
HAS A LOWER
COST PER THOUSAND
AT $ 9.090909091

POST
CPM: $ 9.090909091
ADVERTISING: $ 250
CIRCULATION:   27500

NEWS
```

Sales Required For A Profit

This handy program gives a quick estimate of how many units have to be sold, at a certain "profit" or cashflow amount per unit, to achieve a desired gross profit or cashflow.

Suppose you sell Widgets. Each Widget sold provides a profit of $5. You decide you want an income of $30,000 from selling these Widgets. How many Widgets must you sell? Per year? Per month? Per week? Per day?

By the way, this program assumes a six-day workweek. If you want to use a five-day workweek, change the number 6 at the end of line 70 to 5.

Very handy!

Program Listing

```
10 CALL CLEAR
20 INPUT "INCOME YOU WANT = $":I
30 INPUT "PROFIT PER UNIT SOLD = $":P
40 Y=I/P
50 M=Y/12
60 W=Y/52
70 D=W/6
80 PRINT
90 PRINT
100 PRINT "SELL ";Y;" PER YEAR"
110 PRINT "SELL ";M;" PER MONTH"
120 PRINT "SELL ";W;" PER WEEK"
130 PRINT "SELL ";D;" PER DAY"
140 PRINT
150 PRINT
160 PRINT "TO DO MORE, PRESS ANY KEY"
170 CALL KEY(0,Z,X)
180 IF X=0 THEN 170
190 GOTO 10
```

Sample Run

```
INCOME YOU WANT = $ 30000
PROFIT PER UNIT SOLD = $ 5

SELL  6000   PER YEAR
SELL  500    PER MONTH
SELL  115.3846154  PER WEEK
SELL  19.23076923  PER DAY

TO DO MORE, PRESS ANY KEY
```

Salesman's Commission

Representatives, salesmen, account representatives, sales representatives. Here's the no-sweat way to compute commissions to be paid to your sales corps.

The computer will ask you for pertinent data and then display results including the salesman's name, the pay period, his commission percentage rate, gross sales, and commission payable.

Program Listing

```
10 CALL CLEAR
20 PRINT ">>>>>SALES COMMISSIONS<<<<<"
30 PRINT
40 INPUT "SALES PERIOD ENDING DATE: ":D$
50 INPUT "SALESMAN'S NAME: ":N$
60 INPUT "COMMISSION PERCENTAGE: ":P
70 K=P*0.01
80 INPUT "SALESMAN'S GROSS SALES: $":Q
90 T=K*Q
100 CALL CLEAR
110 PRINT "SALESMAN:     ";N$
120 PRINT "PERIOD END:   ";D$
130 PRINT "PERCENTAGE: ";P;"%"
140 PRINT "GROSS SALES: $";Q
150 PRINT "COMMISSION:   $";T
160 PRINT
```

```
170 PRINT
180 PRINT
190 PRINT "TO DO ANOTHER, PRESS ANY KEY"
200 CALL KEY(0,Z,X)
210 IF X=0 THEN 200
220 K=0
230 T=0
240 CALL CLEAR
250 GOTO 50
```

Sample Run

```
>>>>>SALES COMMISSIONS<<<<<

SALES PERIOD ENDING DATE:  12/31/84
SALESMAN'S NAME: SMITH
COMMISSION PERCENTAGE:   15
SALESMAN'S GROSS SALES: $ 16243

SALESMAN:      SMITH
PERIOD END:    12/31/84
PERCENTAGE:    15 %
GROSS SALES: $ 16243
COMMISSION:  $ 2436.45

TO DO ANOTHER, PRESS ANY KEY
```

Unit Price

Suppose you find 895 green Widgets and buy them for $695. How much did each green Widget cost? Rounded off, $0.78.

Unit price is total price divided by quantity. The quantity can be expressed in weight, total numbers, etc. It works the same whether you are talking about pounds of coffee, yards of concrete, gallons of ice cream, boxes of books, or units of Widgets.

This program asks for the name of the item, quantity purchased and total price paid. It then displays quantity, name, total and unit price.

Program Listing

```
10 CALL CLEAR
20 PRINT "**************"
30 PRINT "* UNIT PRICE *"
40 PRINT "**************"
50 INPUT "NAME OF ITEM: ":N$
60 PRINT "QUANTITY OF ";N$;"S:"
70 INPUT Q
80 PRINT "TOTAL PRICE FOR ALL ";N$;"S:"
90 INPUT P
100 U=P/Q
110 U=INT(100*U+0.5)/100
120 CALL CLEAR
130 PRINT Q;N$;"S TOTAL $";P
140 PRINT " EACH ";N$;" IS $";U
150 FOR L=1 TO 8
160 PRINT
170 NEXT L
180 PRINT "TO DO ANOTHER, PRESS ANY KEY"
190 CALL KEY(0,Z,X)
200 IF X=0 THEN 190
210 U=0
220 GOTO 10
```

Sample Run

```
**************
* UNIT PRICE *
**************
NAME OF ITEM: WIDGET
QUANTITY OF WIDGETS:  895
TOTAL PRICE FOR ALL WIDGETS: $ 695
 895 WIDGETS TOTAL $ 695
 EACH WIDGET IS $ .78

TO DO ANOTHER, PRESS ANY KEY
```

Gross & Net Computer

How much cash flow will I generate if I sell 100 thingamabobs? A question faced everyday in the business office. Whether you sell large lots at wholesale, small quantities across the retail counter, or individual items via mail order, this program will give you a quick estimate of expected cash flow and potential profits.

It allows fast comparisons when quick decisions are needed. The computer asks you questions and then generates the answers you need in an attractive chart.

In response to its inquiries on the display, tell the computer how much it costs to manufacture your thingamabob, what its list price is and at what discount you plan to sell the thingamabobs. As soon as you tell the computer how many thingamabobs you will sell, it will compute the total invoice amount you will charge your customer and your anticipated profits after manufacturing costs are deducted.

This program is a useful tool for small business, whether a local furniture store, supermarket or regional mail-order house.

Program Listing

```
10 CALL CLEAR
20 INPUT "ITEM: ":T$
30 INPUT "LIST PRICE: $":L
40 INPUT "MANUFACTURING COST: $":C
50 INPUT "WHOLESALE DISCOUNT: ":W
60 D=1-0.01*W
70 INPUT "QUANTITY SOLD: ":S
80 I=L*S*D
90 P=I-S*C
100 CALL CLEAR
110 PRINT "ITEM:",T$
120 PRINT "LIST:","$";L
130 PRINT "MFG COST:","$";C
140 PRINT "SOLD:",S
150 PRINT "DISCOUNT:",W;"%"
160 PRINT
170 PRINT "INVOICE:","$";I
180 PRINT "PROFIT:","$";P
190 PRINT
200 PRINT
210 PRINT
```

```
220 INPUT "TO DO MORE, PRESS ENTER":KY$
230 D=0
240 I=0
250 P=0
260 GOTO 10
```

Sample Run

```
ITEM:           WIDGET
LIST PRICE: 0                    $ 9.95
MANUFACTURING COST:              $ 1.35
WHOLESALE DISCOUNT:              50
QUANTITY SOLD:                   500
ITEM:           WIDGET
LIST:       $ 9.95
MFG COST:   $ 1.35
SOLD:         500
DISCOUNT:      50 %

INVOICE:    $ 2487.5
PROFIT:     $ 1812.5

TO DO MORE, PRESS RETURN
```

Selling Prices
Of World Currencies

Your own world currency guide allows you to convert money from one currency to another quickly.

The conversion amounts built into program lines 100 to 590 were selected from the New York City market one day in August 1982. You should check later lists of selling prices and modify the DATA lines (program lines 100 to 590) to show the current, correct amount. Check your local bank or stock broker for the latest exchange rates.

The program will hold even more currencies, if you need them, even in the minimum no-extra-memory-added computer. Of course, you could gain even more bytes of program memory for other use if you used abbreviations for country names or currency names. The problem with such abbreviations is that you have to   remember them later!

As written here, the program includes 50 countries. If you change the total number of countries by changing the DATA lines, be sure to change the number 50 in line 700. The program will run endlessly until you press the BREAK to end it.

Program Listing

```
10 CALL CLEAR
100 DATA ARGENTINA,PESO,.0001
110 DATA AUSTRALIA,DOLLAR,.9815
120 DATA AUSTRIA,SCHILLING,.0584
130 DATA BAHAMAS,DOLLAR,1
140 DATA BELGIUM,FRANC,.0215
150 DATA BELIZE,DOLLAR,.5
160 DATA BERMUDA,DOLLAR,1
170 DATA BRAZIL,CRUZEIEO,.0053
180 DATA CANADA,DOLLAR,.8114
190 DATA CHILE,PESO,.0256
200 DATA CHINA,YUAN,.5236
210 DATA COLOMBIA,PESO,.0256
220 DATA CYPRUS,POUND,2.1552
230 DATA DENMARK,KRONE,.1178
240 DATA ECUADOR,SUCRE,.0303
250 DATA EGYPT,POUND,1.2195
260 DATA FINLAND,MARKKA,.2129
270 DATA FRANCE,FRANC,.1475
280 DATA GERMANY,MARK,.4137
290 DATA GREAT BRITAIN,POUND,1.776
300 DATA GREECE,DRACHMA,.0146
310 DATA HAITI,GOURDE,.2
320 DATA HONG KONG,DOLLAR,.1682
330 DATA HUNGARY,FORINT,.029
340 DATA ICELAND,KRONA,.0994
350 DATA INDIA,RUPEE,.1053
360 DATA IRAQ,DINAR,3.3862
370 DATA IRELAND,POUND,1.4155
380 DATA ISRAEL,SHEKEL,.0377
390 DATA ITALY,LIRA,.0008
400 DATA JAPAN,YEN,.004
```

```
410 DATA MEXICO,PESO,.0111
420 DATA NETHERLANDS,GUILDER,.3781
430 DATA NEW ZEALAND,DOLLAR,.7405
440 DATA NIGERIA,NAIRA,1.4808
450 DATA NORWAY,KRONE,.1523
460 DATA PAKISTAN,RUPEE,.0809
470 DATA PERU,SOL,.0014
480 DATA POLAND,ZLOTY,.0125
490 DATA PORTUGAL,ESCUDO,.0118
500 DATA SUADI ARABIA,RIYAL,.2907
510 DATA SOUTH AFRICA,RAND,.8807
520 DATA SPAIN,PESETA,.0091
530 DATA SWEDEN,KRONA,.1653
540 DATA SWITZERLAND,FRANC,.4902
550 DATA THAILAND,BAHT,.0435
560 DATA TURKEY,LIRA,.0066
570 DATA USSR,RUBLE,1.3986
580 DATA VENEZUELA,BOLIVAR,.2329
590 DATA ZAMBIA,KWACHA,1.084
600 INPUT "COUNTRY: ":C$
700 FOR L=1 TO 50
710 READ CC$
712 READ M$
714 READ V
720 IF CC$=C$ THEN 800
730 CC$=""
740 NEXT L
750 RESTORE
760 GOTO 600
800 RESTORE
810 CALL SOUND(3,1000,1)
820 PRINT M$;" = US$x";V
830 FOR Z=1 TO 11
840 PRINT
850 NEXT Z
860 GOTO 600
```

Sample Run

```
COUNTRY: BELIZE
DOLLAR = US$x .5
```

```
COUNTRY: ZAMBIA
KWACHA = US$x 1.084

COUNTRY: NORWAY
KRONE = US$x .1523

COUNTRY: CANADA
DOLLAR = US$x .8114

COUNTRY: HONG KONG
DOLLAR = US$x .1682

COUNTRY: CHINA
YUAN = US$x .5236
```

Executive Decision Maker

Stumped by a toughie? Got one too hot to handle alone? Need help with major decisions? When there is no other way to decide, punch up this quickie and get a definite YES or NO.

Program Listing

```
10 RANDOMIZE
20 CALL CLEAR
30 R=INT(1000*RND)
40 IF R>499 THEN 70
50 PRINT "NO"
60 GOTO 80
70 PRINT "YES"
80 FOR L=1 TO 10
90 PRINT
100 NEXT L
110 PRINT "TO MAKE ANOTHER"
120 PRINT "IMPORTANT DECISION,"
130 INPUT "PRESS 'ENTER' ":KY$
140 R=0
150 GOTO 20
```